# SCHNITZLER

## BY CARL R. MUELLER

SUSAN C. MOORE, SERIES EDITOR

**PLAYWRIGHTS** in an hour
*know the playwright, love the play*

IN AN HOUR BOOKS • HANOVER, NEW HAMPSHIRE • INANHOURBOOKS.COM
AN IMPRINT OF SMITH AND KRAUS PUBLISHERS, INC • SMITHANDKRAUS.COM

*With grateful thanks to Carl R. Mueller,*
*whose fascinating introductions to his translations*
*of the Greek and German playwrights provided*
*inspiration for this series.*

Published by In an Hour Books
an imprint of Smith and Kraus, Inc.
177 Lyme Road, Hanover, NH 03755
inanhourbooks.com  SmithandKraus.com

Know the playwright, love the play.

In an Hour, In a Minute, and Theater IQ are registered trademarks of
In an Hour Books.

Front cover design by Dan Mehling, dmehling@gmail.com
Text design by Kate Mueller, Electric Dragon Productions
Book production by Dede Cummings Design, DCDesign@sover.net

ISBN-13: 978-1-936232-23-9
ISBN-10: 1-936232-23-5
Library of Congress Control Number: 2009943218

# CONTENTS

# Why Playwrights in an Hour?

This new series by Smith and Kraus Publishers titled Playwrights in an Hour has a dual purpose for being: one academic, the other general. For the general reader, this volume, as well as the many others in the series, offers in compact form the information needed for a basic understanding and appreciation of the works of each volume's featured playwright. Which is not to say that there don't exist volumes on end devoted to each playwright under consideration. But inasmuch as few are blessed with enough time to read the splendid scholarship that is available, a brief, highly focused accounting of the playwright's life and work is in order. The central feature of the series, a thirty- to forty-page essay, integrates the playwright into the context of his or her time and place. The volumes, though written to high standards of academic integrity, are accessible in style and approach to the general reader as well as to the student and, of course, to the theater professional and theatergoer. These books will serve for the brushing up of one's knowledge of a playwright's career, to the benefit of theater work or theatergoing. The Playwrights in an Hour series represents all periods of Western theater: Aeschylus to Shakespeare to Wedekind to Ibsen to Williams to Beckett, and on to the great contemporary playwrights who continue to offer joy and enlightenment to a grateful world.

*Carl R. Mueller*
*School of Theater, Film and Television*
*Department of Theater*
*University of California, Los Angeles*

# Introduction

A rthur Schnitzler is the most precarious of playwrights, sus-
pended as he is between the confident assurance of European
Classicism and the skeptical vertigo of Modernism. At times, his
plays display the conventions of French farce or nineteenth-century
melodrama, in the style of his Hungarian contemporary, Ferenc Molnar.
At the next moment, they plunge us into the dizzying whirlpools of Luigi
Pirandello or the sexual tidal waves of Frank Wedekind.

Part of Schnitzler's elusiveness can be attributed to the fact that he
was born a Jew during a particularly anti-Semitic period in European
history. Coming upon the scene a few years after Austria had lost its
hegemony and united with Hungary, he died just a few months after
Hitler came to power in Germany. This period, as Amos Elon tells us in
his illuminating book, *The Pity of It All,* was perhaps one of the most trying times in history for Germanic Jewry, who had hitherto enjoyed rela-
tive tolerance and respect. And it helped shape his ethnic consciousness
when other Jews, Felix Mendelssohn and Heinrich Heine for example,
were ignoring their heritage and becoming Lutherans.

Like Sigmund Freud, Schnitzler was a physician who specialized in
psychiatry, the insights of which play a large role in his work. And like
that other medical man of the theater, Anton Chekhov, he was fascinated
with class differences, and diagnosed human behavior as being shaped
by similar motivations. But perhaps the dramatist with whom Schnitzler
shared the most common ground was August Strindberg, particularly in
their common emphasis on human sexuality and their mutual belief that
it was in the nature of humankind (or rather women in the case of Strindberg) to be sexually unfaithful.

Both in *La Ronde (Reigen )* and his *Anatol* plays, for example,
Schnitzler focuses exclusively on sexual infidelity. *La Ronde* is virtually a
merry-go-round of promiscuity since each of its ten scenes begins and

ends with a switch of sexual partners, just as each of the seven *Anatol* one-acts concludes with the advent of sexual intercourse. It was partly because of this erotic emphasis that Schnitzler's plays were so often banned or censored or labeled as "Jewish filth," even though by today's standards they seem relatively tame (the lights usually dim before any sexual act is consummated).

Schnitzler's influence on contemporary theater has been subtle but persistent. Although his plays are seldom produced, they are often adapted. For example, in 1991 Larry Gelbart converted *La Ronde* into a satiric political comedy called *Power Failure*, while Stanley Kubrick used Schnitzler's novel *Traumnovelle* as the basis for his last movie, filmed in 1999, called *Eyes Wide Shut*. (I suspect Adrian Lyne's 2002 movie *Unfaithful* with Diane Lane also owes a debt to a Schnitzler work, *Liebelei.*) Arthur Schnitzler remains one of our most underappreciated playwrights despite incisions into the human heart that remain sharp and penetrating.

*Robert Brustein*
*Founding Director of the Yale and American Repertory Theatres*
*Distinguishing Scholar in Residence, Suffolk University*

# Schnitzler

# IN A MINUTE

| AGE | DATE | |
|-----|------|---|
| – | 1862 | **Enter Arthur Schnitzler.** |
| 3 | 1865 | The Klu Klux Klan is founded in Pulaski, Tennessee. |
| 5 | 1867 | Karl Marx — *Das Kapital,* Volume I |
| 9 | 1871 | British Parliament legalizes labor unions. |
| 14 | 1876 | Bulgarians revolt against Ottoman rule in April Uprising. |
| 17 | 1879 | Henrik Ibsen — *A Doll's House* |
| 18 | 1880 | Fyodor Dostoevsky —*The Brothers Karamazov* |
| 22 | 1884 | Berlin Conference launches European scramble for Africa. |
| 27 | 1889 | Gustav Mahler conducts Symphony No. 1 in Budapest premiere. |
| **29** | **1891** | **Arthur Schnitzler — *The Adventure of His Life*** |
| 30 | 1892 | Oscar Wilde — *Lady Windermere's Fan* |
| **33** | **1896** | **Arthur Schnitzler — *Questioning Fate*** |
| 34 | 1897 | The Vienna Secessionists, like Gustav Klimt, promote Art Nouveau. |
| **36** | **1899** | **Arthur Schnitzler — *The Green Cockatoo*** |
| **38** | **1900** | **Arthur Schnitzler — *The Veil of Beatrice*** |
| 39 | 1901 | August Strindberg — *The Dance of Death* |
| 40 | 1902 | The teddy bear makes its debut. |
| **42** | **1904** | **Arthur Schnitzler — *The Lonely Way*** |
| 43 | 1905 | Einstein formulates Special Theory of Relativity. |
| 46 | 1908 | London hosts the fourth modern Olympic Games. |
| 47 | 1909 | Women are admitted to German universities. |
| 51 | 1913 | Henry Ford pioneers the assembly line in his automotive factory. |
| 55 | 1917 | Russian Revolution annihilates czarist autocracy in Moscow. |
| 56 | 1918 | Habsburg Empire falls and Austria becomes a republic. |
| 58 | 1920 | Women take on a sexy, sleek, and boyish image in film, *The Flapper.* |
| 60 | 1922 | Ghandi sentenced to six years in prison by the British Colonial Court. |
| 61 | 1923 | Hitler's Beer Hall Putsch |
| **64** | **1926** | **Arthur Schnitzler — *New Year's Eve*** |
| 67 | 1929 | Sigmund Freud — *Civilization and Its Discontents* |
| **69** | **1931** | **Exit Arthur Schnitzler.** |

A snapshot of the playwright's world. From historical events to pop-culture and the literary landscape of the time, this brief list catalogues events that directly or indirectly impacted the playwright's writing. Play citations refer to opening or premiere dates.

# Schnitzler

# HIS WORKS

## DRAMATIC WORKS

*Paracelsus*

*Anatol*

*Flirtation (Liebelei)*

*The Green Cockatoo*

*La Ronde*

*Living Hours*

*The Lonely Way*

*The Road into the Open*

*Countess Mizzi*

*Young Medardus*

*The Undiscovered Country*

*Professor Bernhardi*

*Comedy of Words*

*Comedy of Seduction*

*Therese*

## SHORT STORIES AND NOVELLAS

*Dying*

*Lieutenant Gustl*

*Blind Geronimo and His Brother*

*Bert*

*The Prophecy*

*Casanova's Homecoming*

*Fräulein Else*

---

This section presents a complete list of the playwright's works in chronological order. Titles appearing in another language indicate that they were first written and premiered in that language.

*Dream Story*
*Night Games*
*Flight into Darkness*

## NONFICTION

*Youth in Vienna*, 1968
*Diary: 1879–1931*

# Onstage with Schnitzler

*Introducing Colleagues and
Contemporaries of Arthur Schnitzler*

 ## THEATER

Anton Chekhov, Russian playwright
Noël Coward, English playwright
Henrik Ibsen, Norwegian playwright
Eugene O'Neill, American playwright
Luigi Pirandello, Italian playwright
Oscar Wilde, Irish playwright
Frank Wedekind, German playwright
William Butler Yeats, Irish poet and playwright

 ## ARTS

Georges Bizet, French composer
Paul Gauguin, French painter
Gustav Klimt, Austrian painter
Gustav Mahler, Austrian composer
Henri Matisse, French painter
Claude Monet, French painter
Auguste Rodin, French sculptor
Arnold Schoenberg, Austrian composer

 ## FILM

Charles Chaplin, English actor and director
Marlene Dietrich, German actress
Walt Disney, American animator and film mogul
Lillian Gish, American actress

---

This section lists contemporaries whom the playwright may or may not have known.

Buster Keaton, American actor and director
Mary Pickford, American actress
Erich Von Stroheim, German director
Mae West, American actress

## POLITICS/ MILITARY

Alfred Dreyfus, French army officer
Franz Ferdinand, Austro-Hungarian archduke
George V, English monarch
Adolf Hitler, Austrian-German dictator
Benito Mussolini, Italian fascist dictator
Nicholas II, Russian czar
Wilhelm II, German emperor and king of Prussia
Woodrow Wilson, American president

## SCIENCE

Jean Martin Charcot, French neurologist
Marie Curie, French scientist
Pierre Curie, French physicist
Charles Darwin, English naturalist
Albert Einstein, German-American physicist
Sigmund Freud, Austrian physician and neurologist
Carl Jung, Swiss psychologist
Richard von Krafft-Ebing, German neurologist
Max Weber, German sociologist

## LITERATURE

Joseph Conrad, English novelist
Fyodor Dostoevsky, Russian novelist
Hermann Hesse, German novelist
Franz Kafka, Austrian-Czech novelist
Guy de Maupassant, French writer
Rainer Maria Rilke, Austro-German poet and dramatist
Leo Tolstoi, Russian novelist
Emile Zola, French novelist

## RELIGION/ PHILOSOPHY

Simone de Beauvoir, French philosopher

Henri Bergson, French philosopher

Albert Camus, French Existentialist philosopher

Benedetto Croce, Italian philosopher and critic

Mohandas K. Gandhi, Indian political and spiritual leader

Karl Marx, German socialist philosopher

Friedrich Nietzsche, German philosopher

Jean-Paul Sartre, French philosopher

## SPORTS

Charlotte Cooper, English tennis player

Dwight F. Davis, American tennis player

W. G. Grace, English cricketer

Thomas King, English boxer

Kid McCoy, American boxer

George Herman "Babe" Ruth, American baseball player

Marie Taglioni, Italian-Swedish ballerina

Cy Young, American baseball player

## BUSINESS/INDUSTRY

Andrew Carnegie, Scottish-American industrialist

William Durant, American founder of GM and Chevrolet

Lewis Edson Waterman, American founder of the Waterman pen
company

Henry Ford, American founder of the Ford Motor Company

King Camp Gillette, American businessman and inventor of the
safety razor

W. K. Kellogg, American industrialist and founder of Kellogg

J. P. Morgan, American financier

John D. Rockefeller, American industrialist

# SCHNITZLER

in an hour

## PRELIMINARIES

The Austrian playwright Arthur Schnitzler (1862–1931) is one of the seminal forces in both German-speaking and world drama. He was in every sense a total man of letters: playwright, novelist, and short-story writer. But he was also a physician, and perhaps this is the basis for his acute perception into the mind and soul of *fin-de-siècle* Vienna — Vienna at the end of the nineteenth century.

## EDUCATION AND FREUD

Schnitzler's father, a well-known Jewish throat specialist who founded a leading medical journal of the day, deeply influenced him to enter the medical profession. He studied at the University of Vienna, from which he graduated in 1885 with a dissertation on the hypnotic treatment of neurosis. Even after he began his literary career (against his father's objections), Schnitzler continued to review medical publications on such topics as hysteria, hypnosis, sexual pathology, and

---

This is the core of the book. The essay places the playwright in the context of his or her world and analyzes the influences and inspirations within that world.

psychotherapy. These studies provided Schnitzler with the tools to dissect his characters as incisively as if he were conducting a delicate surgical operation.

Sigmund Freud, whose clinical interests paralleled those of Schnitzler, was living in Vienna at the same time. In 1906, Schnitzler sent a fiftieth-birthday greeting to Freud — their first contact. Freud wrote back, noting the "extensive concurrence" that existed between their views on psychology and eroticism. He wrote how much he deeply admired Schnitzler's writing and was delighted to learn that Schnitzler had drawn inspiration from his own work.

Freud, in fact, some years later, in 1922, called Schnitzler "my *doppelgänger,*" or double, and for good reason. As Frederic Morton points out in *A Nervous Splendor: Vienna 1888–1889*, the two were not only contemporaries but fellow Jews and students at the same university. They were both physicians and devotees of hypnotism. But most tellingly of all was their parallel interest in the tension between the individual's inner motives and desires and the social façade he or she presents to the world.

As it happened, they met only a few times, though they lived within walking distance of each other. It has been suggested that Schnitzler the doctor and Freud with his artist's imagination were too similar for comfort. They could never be close and were content to maintain a respectful distance. Both Freud's psychoanalytic work and Schnitzler's literary output were inextricably linked with the social and intellectual milieu of their time.

## VIENNA: HARBINGER OF MODERNISM

Turn-of-the-century Vienna, appropriately known as the City of Dreams, produced such a rich cultural flowering that one has to look back to Athens in the mid-fifth century BCE to find its equal. The Austro-Hungarian Empire, the *Donaumonarchie* (monarchy on the Danube), was declining, and an end-of-the-century atmosphere of decadence and pleasure seeking was dominant. And yet, intellectually and culturally, Vienna had never been more vital.

A spirit of innovation was present in turn-of-the-century Vienna. The visual artists Gustav Klimt and Egon Schiele, reacting in part against the decorative art of Hans Makart, paved the way for Expressionism. In music, Gustav Mahler, considered one of the most important late-Romantic/early-Modernist composers, and Anton Bruckner, with his rich harmonies, were laying the foundation for the later free tonal explorations of Schoenberg, Webern, and Berg.

Concurrent with all this artistic ferment, Freud was busy splitting the psyche into conscious and unconscious, superego, ego, and id. The function of dreams, the causes of hysteria, and theories of sexuality were brought forward for consideration.

New? Yes. Exciting? Yes. But Freud was not officially recognized by the medical establishment, and the Viennese middle classes were outraged by the sexual implications of his findings. Similarly, the general public was largely hostile to the avant-garde work of Vienna's writers, composers, and visual artists. Klimt, Schiele, Mahler, and Bruckner, along with architects Otto Wagner and Adolf Loos and a host of others, were not welcomed. The mainstream intelligentsia much preferred the safe, light music of Johann Strauss and the ornate decorative art of Makart.

It was in this context of conservative status quo and artistic innovation that Schnitzler wrote with charm and grace and, more important, great compassion.

## ESCAPING BOURGEOIS PROPRIETY

Schnitzler was not the only young writer seeking to escape the constraints of middle-class life and attitudes. In the final decade of the century, a group of young authors banded together, meeting in one of Vienna's social institutions — the coffeehouse. Here they were able to escape their restrictive, proper bourgeois upbringing. The Jung Wien

(Young Vienna), as they were called, met regularly from 1890 to 1897. In addition to Schnitzler, their membership included Hermann Bahr, Hugo von Hofmannsthal, Richard Beer-Hofmann, Karl Kraus, Peter Altenberg, and Leopold von Andrian. Together, they formed a literary circle whose interests were primarily cultural; they took little notice of political developments in Vienna or elsewhere.

Jung Wien was, without question, a socially significant group of young writers from upper-middle-class and even aristocratic families. Schnitzler, while not of the aristocracy, was scarcely out of place given his family's position in society. He was the son of a wealthy professional father, a student at Vienna's University, and, for a short time, an officer cadet in the Imperial Army. As such, he had every opportunity to take part in the pleasure-seeking lifestyle of the privileged. At the same time, he continued his medical practice until, with the death of his father in 1892, he was able to devote himself fulltime to literature, becoming an effective critic and chronicler of Viennese society.

## VIENNA AND THE JEWS

Austria has always been an overwhelmingly Catholic country, with the presence of Jews considered a thorn in its side. For centuries, according to Peter Gay in his *Schnitzler's Century*, "Christians had scorned, or at least isolated, Jews as the killers of Christ, desecrators of holy objects, and (in the muddled minds of fanatics including some princes of the church) slaughterers of Christian babies to draw their blood for making the Passover matzoh." These "primitive slanders," according to Peter Gay, continued to have some appeal among the uneducated well into the nineteenth century, though they were beginning to lose support in the "light of increased worldliness, fading piety, and the assimilationist ideals of the Enlightenment."

Losing support, yes, but not disappearing. Pogroms (which literally means to "wreak havoc") were organized massacres of people, particularly Jews, and continued well into Victorian times. These pogroms, Western European commentators were quick to point out, happened only in Russia, not in the "advanced" countries of Britain, France, and the Low Countries. According to these commentators, Russia was the site of the 1881 pogroms because it was a backward country with an undeveloped political culture, unlike the countries of Western Europe. But, as Gay notes, the Dreyfus affair in France in 1895 soon showed how self-delusional this complacent analysis was. Alfred Dreyfus, a young Jewish officer, was unjustly accused of treason and hurriedly court-martialed. He was eventually exonerated, but not before becoming the scapegoat of virulent anti-Semitism in France and suffering imprisonment for five years. Schnitzler followed the case closely and was a vigorous defender of Dreyfus.

Gay notes that the sudden rise in anti-Semitism in Austria dominated Schnitzler's young adult years. While Schnitzler was attending gymnasium (1871–79), his Jewishness was not an issue and presented few problems. He made the following entry in his journal about his years at the gymnasium:

> During my Gymnasium years, [anti-Semitism] scarcely felt. The first who was considered an anti-Semite, or, since the word didn't exist in those days, a *Judenfresser* (Jew devourer) was a certain Deperis, who wouldn't speak to a Jew, but was considered ridiculous by his Gentile colleagues. He was very elegant, didn't have to pay for his tuition, was stupid and today enjoys the title of Privy Councilor. Among the professors — Professor Blume, still relatively harmless. A moderately gifted man, Wagnerian, very German-national, pronounces all Jewish names with derision but is not unfair in his behavior toward his Jewish pupils. Marries a Jewess.

It was as a student in the School of Medicine at the University of Vienna (1879–85) that Schnitzler met anti-Semitism in a harsher form, as he recorded in his posthumously published autobiography, *Jugend in Wien (My Youth in Vienna)*.

The question was very real at that time for us young people, especially for those of us who were Jews, since anti-Semitism began to flourish and was becoming increasingly virulent in student circles. The German Nationalist fraternities had begun by expelling all Jews and Jewish descendants from their midst. . . . One of the Jewish students who belonged to a German nationalist fraternity . . . was Theodor Herzl. I myself saw him parading around in the ranks of his fraternity brothers with his blue fraternity cap and black cane with the ivory handle on which the FVC (*floreat vivat crescat* [meaning "flourish, live, grow"]) was engraved. That they expelled him from their midst for being Jewish undoubtedly was the initial motivation that transformed the German nationalist student and spokesman in the academic debating hall (where without knowing each other personally, we had stared at each other mockingly one evening at a meeting) into a perhaps more enthusiastic than convinced Zionist, as which he continues to live on in posterity.

Theodor Herzl, a journalist and playwright in Vienna, later became a leading spokesman for Zionism and is known as the father of Zionism. He concluded, after witnessing the Dreyfus affair and other anti-Semitic incidents, that assimilation would not solve the problem of anti-Semitism and that only the establishment of a Jewish state would provide the Jewish people with the necessary international clout.

Schnitzler noticed with dismay that anti-Semitism was becoming a force in politics and even in his upper-class social circles. Sometime around 1912, Schnitzler made the following journal entry:

It was not possible, especially not for a Jew in public life, to ignore the fact that he was a Jew; nobody else was doing so, not the Gentiles and even less the Jews. You had the choice of being counted as insensitive, obtrusive, and fresh; or of being oversensitive, shy, and suffering from feelings of persecution. And even if you managed somehow to conduct yourself so that nothing showed, it was possible to remain completely untouched; as for instance a person may not remain unconcerned whose skin has been anesthetized but who has to watch, with his eyes open, how it is scratched by an unclean knife, even cut into until the blood flows.

Reinhard Urbach, in his book *Arthur Schnitzler*, notes, correctly, that Schnitzler never avoided the Jewish problem but always identified himself as an Austrian writer.

## INTELLECTUAL FOMENT VERSUS POLITICAL STAGNATION

Bruce Thompson, in his *Schnitzler's Vienna*, writes of how Austria was politically weakened and unstable after its defeat in the Austro-Prussian War of 1866; it was no longer considered an important international player. In 1867, the Austrian Empire was divided between Hungary and Austria and became known as the Austro-Hungarian Empire. The Austrian House of Habsburg ruled over the western and northern parts of the former Austrian Empire, with Vienna as its capital. Vienna became a melting pot of racial and political ideas, further destabilizing the weakened government. As Thompson notes, "Pan-Germanism, Pan-Slavism, Marxism, Christian Socialism, Zionism all coincided at the heart of the Habsburg Empire in the years of its decline, and by the end of the century the stability of the empire was threatened by numerous mutually hostile factions."

But the Austro-Hungarian Empire, for all the artistic and intel-lectual foment within it, was politically stagnant as well as weak. The spirit of change, so vitally needed in the empire, was static in Viennese society, whereas elsewhere in Europe, artists and intellectuals were profoundly engaged in social reforms. Though Viennese artists and intellectuals wanted to alter the status quo, they felt trapped in their culture and isolated from the rest of Europe, unable to ally themselves with the broader social and political activity of the continent. Schnitzler, like his contemporaries in Vienna, felt cut off from the liberating trends in the rest of Europe. As Martin Swales, in *Arthur Schnitzler: A Critical Study*, notes:

> Schnitzler comes from the kind of social and intellectual background that would normally provide the core of enlightened liberalism within the political spectrum of the time. And yet the social and political stagnation proves too strong; the liberalism atrophies into passivity and skepticism. And Schnitzler's situation could be paralleled over and over again in the intellectual life of contemporary Vienna. And it is important to note that even at a much lower social level the same kind of hopelessness and weariness prevails.

## EVERY CLASS IN ITS PLACE — MOSTLY

Important, too, in understanding *fin-de-siècle* Vienna is the highly structured nature of its society. Every class had its position and identity, and it was expected that no one would stray from his or her place in society. As Thompson points out, at the top of the pyramid was the aristocracy at home in the palace of the inner city; then the diplomatic circles at home in the third district; the industrialists and merchants in the Ring area; the lower middle classes in the inner districts; and finally, the proletariat in the outer suburbs.

But upward social mobility was not unheard of. An actress, the daughter of a shopkeeper, becomes the longtime confidant of the emperor, and a butcher shop attendant from the suburbs becomes the owner of the prestigious Sacher Hotel across from the Imperial Opera House; but "at the very top of the social hierarchy the families of the older, highly privileged nobility led an artificial, exclusive existence, dividing their time between their residences in Vienna and their country estates."

But they were not the only "exclusive, privileged caste"; so too were the officers of Emperor Franz Josef's Imperial Army. Though the army was expensive and inefficient, the citizenry was fond of it, and society indulged the officers. They lived by their own code of honor and operated outside civil law. Dueling was illegal for civilians and punishable by imprisonment, but an officer whose honor had been attacked could demand a duel. Conversely, if he refused a challenge to a duel, he could be stripped of his commission.

Apart from such privileged groups, Vienna in 1900 was largely a bourgeois city, its wealth having been made in the 1870s, when large middle-class businesses were founded and fortunes were made. Schnitzler himself was reared in a prosperous middle-class family, culturally and intellectually sophisticated and devoted to the arts, in particular the theater. His father, a laryngologist, had many famous performing artists for patients.

## JUDGING FROM A DISTANCE

Through Schnitzler's work, one can "read" the Vienna of his time. But he is not simply uncritically reporting what he observes nor does he subscribe to the social codes of his time. Swales observes that some commentators "have restricted his human and artistic range by identifying him with the kind of social world he describes. In so doing, they have overlooked the degree to which he stands apart from and judges the experience which he so penetratingly evokes." On the other hand, he is more concerned with individual behavior than with social movements. As Swales notes, Schnitzler has little to say about the political issues of his day; his plays are all about the individual. These characters do not identify themselves with any social group, and nearly all of them are people from his class — prosperous, upper class, and educated. Still, as Swales notes, he manages in this restricted world he creates to "give — at his best — a remarkably suggestive portrait of the intellectual climate of his times, of the problematic areas of social, moral, aesthetic, philosophical thinking which were of such concern for his contemporaries. What interests Schnitzler most is not society as such, but the kind of psychological situation which individual participation in that society produces."

Schnitzler is the biographer of an age that has passed; but this age continues to fire the imagination and interest of the present. Today, we see turn-of-the-century Vienna as the crucible of all that is modern. In this repressive, dream-oriented, and reality-hating city, modernism hit with a vengeance — like the Freudian id revolting against the authoritarian superego of the Austrian monarchy, with its unhealthy clinging to tradition. Schnitzler's contribution to our understanding of that fascinating and troublesome period cannot be overestimated.

## THE SUN THAT MIGHT NOT RISE

Schnitzler's characters, just like their living prototypes, are determined to squeeze every drop of sensual gratification from life. Yet at their back hovers the Angel of Death, that Baroque morality figure, poised to descend. Life can be snuffed out in a single moment. In his plays, Schnitzler embodies the Angel of Death in many forms. In *Flirtation* (*Liebelei*), the angel is the austere, foreboding, and judgmental husband of Fritz's mistress. In *La Ronde* (*Reigen*), it is the omnipresent fear that tomorrow's sun may never rise. In *Anatol*, his cycle of one-act plays, it is time that is relentless and waits for no man; the moment is all. Sex in Schnitzler's plays is often frenetic. Through their constant indulgence in sex, his characters desperately attempt to avoid the realization that their life lived solely for pleasure is empty and that society is crumbling all around them. The characters in Schnitzler's plays are like aristocratic ostrichs with their heads in the sand.

In every way, Schnitzler's plays portray the Vienna in which he lived and wrote. One of the few remaining Baroque cities of the world, Vienna still lived the Baroque tradition and set itself apart from modernization; it resisted both the railroad and the telephone. In the

City of Dreams, people suffered repression and were compensated for it like no place else. Is it any wonder that Vienna is the city in which Sigmund Freud formulated his theory of hysteria? By studying hysteria in his patients, Freud was in reality identifying the psychosis of the society in which he lived and worked. Where else but in the City of Dreams could his epic work *The Interpretation of Dreams* have been written? Had psychoanalysis developed anywhere but Vienna, it might well have taken another form. Freud's final transcendent works condemning civilization — *The Future of an Illusion* and *Civilization and Its Discontents* — hold the mirror up to us all but especially to the citizens of Vienna at the turn of the nineteenth century. Like Freud, Schnitzler also holds up a mirror to his age and his society. If much in his plays and the narrative seems sentimental, even precious, it is so by careful design: Beneath that fun-loving exterior of whirling waltzes lurk cruelty, duplicity, bitterness, ruthlessness, skepticism, and, ultimately, despair.

## ILLUSION AND REALITY

One of Schnitzler's principal themes is the confusion between reality and illusion, much like that of Luigi Pirandello, a contemporary of Schnitzler's. As in the Italian playwright's work, illusion is the one sure means of escaping reality and one's inability to cope with it. Illusion is at best a veil, and at worst, it shuts the eyes entirely. At the end of *The Undiscovered Country (Das Weite Land)*, Friedrich tells Erna, who is trying to convince him that they must be together, that what she feels is illusory. He tells her that "everything is an illusion," which suggests that illusion inevitably reverses itself into hard, cruel reality.

## REACHING THE INNER SPACES

Schnitzler devoted his art solely to the close study of individuals. This focus automatically eliminated, except on rare occasion, scenes involving groups. When a small group was unavoidable, he broke up the group into two-character scenes. This concentration allowed Schnitzler to use the techniques of depth psychology to reach the inner spaces of his characters.

Urbach makes a shrewd observation when he writes that "the phenomenon of the mass [in Schnitzler] is reduced to the typical in the individual," without ever losing sight of the individual. His characters are both identifiable types and individuals. Urbach notes it is easy to reveal the weaknesses associated with a type. But by creating an individual and insightfully probing his or her psychology, Schnitzler makes the character's weaknesses more understandable. It is harder, then, to judge and moralize. Moralizing is not an overt part of Schnitzler's dramatic vocabulary.

# ANATOL

*Anatol* is Schnitzler's first major attempt at dramatic writing, and it might well be considered his most charming. Neither planned nor composed as a whole, *Anatol* was written scene by scene between 1888 and 1892; each scene premiered independently. This series of seven one-acts is loosely united by the character of Anatole, a young Viennese sensualist. In each scene, Anatol is with a different mistress. Together, these seven short, episodic scenes present a picture of a tired and fading society finding escape in an eternal round of erotic encounters. *Anatol*'s eroticism is light and uncomplicated, romantic in a distinctly late-nineteenth-century Viennese manner. Sex is more implied than outright; it will happen, to be sure, but sweetly offstage, never on. Sex in *Anatol* is also infused with humor and gentility; something that will happen, and then fade, and when it fades, there will be another episode to take its place after a little time to recover. *Anatol* is gentler in tone and mode than the more clinical, coldly unsentimental *La Ronde*, but it is no less ironic in its depiction of the futile search for sexual gratification. Though sweetness may always promise to be around the next corner, each successive affair is destined for failure and disillusionment. In Schnitzler, the expectations of the young woman, or Viennese Sweet Young Thing (*süsse Mädel*), are seldom met because of the egocentric needs of the man, who only seeks a little diversion from his state of boredom and wants to avoid any serious entanglements. The disappointment on both sides is equally comic and tragic and therefore sad — but, implies Schnitzler, that's life.

## Love as Diversion

The so-called battle of the sexes is here more a game than anything else: a fencing match with rapiers blunted so that no one really gets hurt. Along with Anatol is his sidekick, Max, who appears in five of the play's seven scenes. It is he who plays Mephisto to Anatol's Faust; the realist to his friend's fashionable romantic dissatisfaction. Max is the sounding board for Anatol's delusions of grandeur. "I thought," boasts Anatol, "of myself as one of the great men of history. Those girls and women — I ground them underfoot as I strode across the earth. I thought of it as a law of nature. My way lies over these bodies." To which Max replies with no small sense of irony though no less a sense of humor: "The storm wind that scatters the blossoms." At which point, Anatol becomes just another guy — at least for a while.

Throughout the seven episodes, Anatol, like men always and forever, must believe that he is the motivating factor in each of his affairs. Schnitzler, however, being a wise sensualist himself, makes it very clear that it is generally Anatol's women who come out ahead when the accounts are finally reckoned. Anatol is not built to be a long-term lover, one who provides a secure base and inspires confidence in women; instead, he is ill at ease with stability. As with many of his fellow rich young Viennese men about town, he is superficial, depleted, empty — as empty as the society crumbling about him. He is not out for love, but for diversion, and he must be in charge of it — or think he is. He must call the shots. In "Farewell Supper," he has invited Annie, a member of the ballet chorus at the Imperial Opera, to a late supper in a private dining room of the elegant Sacher Hotel. He has decided that their affair has gone on long enough and it is time to move on; he needs another diverting affair to free him from his enervating boredom. But before Anatol can tell Annie of his decision, she informs him that she has struck up an affair (that she swears is love) with a young man from the chorus and this will be her and Anatol's last meeting. Anatol is outraged, of course, but, more properly, humiliated that one of his "diversions" should have won out at his game, one at which only the male is meant to win.

## Asking the Big Question

Anatol is also a young man who doesn't live fully in reality, but does everything in his power to hide inside illusion. In the first scene, "Questioning Fate," Anatol and Max are discussing one of the major topics in turn-of-the-century Vienna, hypnotism, a subject both Freud and Schnitzler wrote about early in their medical careers. Anatol is forever expressing his frustration that his love interests are unfaithful. "Women are unfaithful," he complains to Max. "It's their nature. And they don't even realize it. I read two or three books at once. They have two or three love affairs at once."

Max, however, suggests that Anatol hypnotize his current diversion and ask her the big question, which can only yield the truth. Anatol agrees. Cora arrives. Cora agrees to being hypnotized, not knowing the ulterior motive. With Max out of the room, Anatol edges closer and closer to the big moment, the sealing of his fate, but at the last moment fails to ask it. When Max returns and learns of Anatol's fear he castigates him:

> Anatol! You have the opportunity to resolve the enigma that
> the world's wisest men have beaten their heads over! If only

you'd ask the question. *One question* will tell you whether you are among the few who are loved exclusively by one woman; the identity of your rival in love; and by what means he succeeded. And yet you refuse! You have the power to question fate! But you *won't*! The truth is at your fingertips! And you do nothing! Do you know why? Because the woman you love is the same as you suppose all women to be. And because illusion is a thousand times more dear to you than the truth. Let's stop this. Wake her up, and be satisfied that — that you might have accomplished a miracle.

In this lovely moment, delicately handled by the playwright, Schnitzler illustrates Anatol's weakness, his inability to see the truth. But Schnitzler had something else in mind: he was writing not just about Anatol, the individual man, but about the society that Anatol lives in. Schnitzler is a miniaturist. He makes his points through the individuals, through personal exchanges, not through verbal debate, as say, George Bernard Shaw does in his plays. Anatol stands for the Viennese aristocracy, who bury their heads in the sand and refuse to acknowledge reality.

## FLIRTATION

*Flirtation*, written in 1895 under the untranslatable title *Liebelei*, centers around Christine, a young, gentle, and sensitive girl of the lower middle class. She falls in love with Fritz, a dashing, wealthy young Viennese man about town. She makes the mistake of taking her lover and their affair seriously, rather than as a passing fancy. Her tragedy is that she fails to play the game of love according to the well-established rules of the period. It is her first time, and she commits herself all the way, both physically and emotionally.

Fritz has been having an affair with an upper-class married woman. His best friend, Theodore (Max of *Anatol* under another name), has suggested that Fritz end the affair and find a less serious successor. He thinks Fritz has been taking his affair with the married woman too seriously — even to the point of considering eloping. Unbeknownst to Fritz, Theodore has arranged for Fritz to meet Christine, a friend of Theodore's current lover, Mitzi, at Fritz's apartment. Christine, thinks Theodore, will help Fritz out of his present involvement. As the play opens, the two couples have gathered together at the apartment. Fritz and Christine become lovers, but Christine is unaware of Fritz's recent affair with the married woman. Later, the married woman's husband appears and challenges Fritz to a duel. Fritz accepts and is killed. Christine, having believed in his love for her, realizes too late that it was an illusion and that she was merely a pastime, and she commits suicide at Fritz's grave.

## Not Beyond the Pleasure Principle

*Flirtation*, for all its delicacy, is a hard-hitting piece of theater. It's a good example of how Schnitzler manages to criticize aspects of his society without moralizing or being didactic. He has sympathy for both sides and allows the situation to speak for itself.

To this end, he structures his plot around two couples, Theodore and Mitzi and Fritz and Christine. The plot's thrust or, in playwriting terms, its through-line, is an examination of the game of love. Theodore and Mitzi represent the norm of the time. Theodore sees nothing wrong in having brief, inconsequential love affairs; he begins and ends them with ease. For him, it's natural and expected that lower-class women from the Vorstadt, an area just outside Vienna, are willing to be lovers with upper-class men, at the same time understanding that the relationship is for amusement only. Mitzi understands and accepts their casual relationship and is content to keep it superficial.

This, then, is *Liebelei*, the game of love, an unspoken mutual agreement to please the senses in every way possible without a thought that it might be serious or emotional. Theodore says as much to Fritz in Act One when warning him about the affair with the married woman. It makes Theodore nervous to see his friend Fritz getting too emotionally entangled with someone. He encourages Fritz to distract himself from the married woman by having an affair with Christine. Fritz, to his credit, is momentarily uncertain; he says that Christine is "just too good" for him. But he eventually agrees to take up with her, simply as way to recover from his adulterous affair.

## Revolting Against Convention

The two central characters of the play are, of course, Fritz and Christine. Unlike Theodore and Mitzi, they refuse, or are simply unable, to conform to the social norm, the game of *Liebelei*. Theodore warns Fritz of the practical dangers of a relationship with a married woman — the danger of tripping up in any number of ways, through letters, gifts, and meetings at his apartment and elsewhere; the danger of a suspicious and jealous husband who might harm him. But most dangerous of all is to fall in love and into the trap of taking the affair seriously, which is precisely what Fritz has been doing with the married woman.

But he evidently also falls in love with Christine, even though she was intended to be only a diversion. We see as much when, the day before the duel with the husband (that Angel of Death that frequently appears in Schnitzler's work), Fritz visits Christine at her father's house in the Vorstadt and displays genuine concern for her — for her interests, her life, her well-being. Perhaps his realization that he might not survive the duel has made him more sensitive, more present. That scene between them, even though part of it is a lie, allows Christine a glimpse of the kind of intimacy that she has been searching for all along, but has not found, even with Fritz.

Later, when Christine finds out about Fritz's death, her response is violent and passionate, a revolt against the social conventions. She learns that she wasn't Fritz's prime love, that she was nothing more than a pastime, and that he left no letter, no message for her. He is gone from her life, and she has nothing to remember him by, no sign that she meant anything to him. Not only that, she has been deprived of seeing his body, and her very existence is hidden from his relatives. With fierce passion, she protests the role imposed on her, as a lower-class woman. Her act tears a rent so wide in the curtain of bourgeois respectability that it can never again be mended.

## LA RONDE

*La Ronde*, Schnitzler's most famous play, is an incisive picture of its time. Banned and censored when it first came out, it's now considered a masterpiece of drama, a hard-hitting psychological and sociological criticism of his time.

The complete *La Ronde* cycle (*Reigen* in German), written between 1897 and 1899 and commercially published in 1903, was not given its German-language premiere until 1920 in Berlin. Before that, in 1900, feeling the play was highly susceptible to misinterpretation, Schnitzler had it privately printed in an edition of 200 copies, for distribution to friends. Yet, as copies were transferred from one individual to another, it soon became a literary sensation. And with the 1903 publication, it was summarily attacked as subversive and obscene. The press refused to review it; the police stopped a public reading in Vienna; and Germany confiscated and banned the publication. When an unauthorized production was mounted in Budapest in 1912, it was offensively and tastelessly performed and consequently banned by the police. The play caused subsequent riots in Munich and Berlin, occasioned a trial, and was even discussed in the Austrian Parliament. Finally, in 1921, it received its Viennese première, causing further demonstrations, including proto-Nazi protests that it was "Jewish filth."

# Enemy Time

The play is a series of ten dialogues, each between a man and a woman and each leading to sexual intercourse. The ten participants bridge the entire range of Viennese society, from the Prostitute, to the Soldier, the Parlor Maid, the Young Gentleman, the Young Wife, the Husband, the Sweet Young Thing, the Poet, the Actress, and the Count. Beginning with the Prostitute and the Soldier, each successive scene uses the person of the higher class from the scene before. Thus the second scene engages the Soldier and the Parlor Maid, and the third the Parlor Maid and the Young Gentleman, and so on. In the final scene the Count and the Prostitute of Scene One are brought together: The highest and lowest are reduced to a common denominator.

It would be easy to say that *Anatol*, with its loosely connected scenes, served as a training ground for *La Ronde*, but that would be far from the truth. Each dialogue in *La Ronde* is a different take on society. In both *Anatol* and *Flirtation*, sex, or love, is a frivolous, superficial game to pass the time. *Anatol* is a nostalgic, gentle, almost romantic picture of its society, whereas *La Ronde* is considerably harsher and more cynical. Time, too, takes on a darker hue; no longer are the characters passing time merely to escape the boredom of a dying society. Time is now spelled with a capital T because it is always present, in the shadows, ready to annihilate.

In the first scene, the Prostitute's admonition to the Soldier she is trying to lure into sex is: "Come on. Don't go. We could be dead tomorrow." And with each scene, as the social standing of the participants rises, the presence and threat of Time becomes stronger and more urgent. The effect of Time on the play's characters, from the bottom of the social scale to the top, is to make them more greedy for sex and pleasure — to the virtual annihilation of the other. In each scene, however, the female partner seeks duration and something meaningful, a slowing down of Time; whereas the male drives fiercely onward to the conclusion as though he fears Time will catch him before he can escape Time. This never results in love, only animal passion.

## *THE GREEN COCKATOO*

*The Green Cockatoo (Der grüne Kakadu)*, a play in one act, is a prime example of Schnitzler playing with Pirandellian illusion and reality. The play takes place in a sordid Paris tavern in 1789, on the night of the storming of the Bastille. Various actors from local theaters are performing impromptu scenes of crime for the pleasure of the slumming Parisian aristocracy. One actor tells of pickpockets at work outside; another relates how he set fire to a house; a third tells how he came upon a murder. The host of the tavern tells his noble guests that they are all rogues and pigs and says he hopes they are next in line for execution. No one knows whether he is acting for the gentry's delight or if he is serious.

Henri, a good-natured actor, reveals to the shuddering guests how he has just murdered a nobleman who was his wife's lover. The host of the tavern knows that Henri's wife really did have an affair; what the host does not know is whether Henri is acting or telling the truth. As it happens, Henri is only acting, but not for long, for he soon learns the truth, and when that same nobleman enters the tavern, Henri stabs him to death. In the ensuing horror and confusion, the stormers of the Bastille rush in, and the frightened gentry flee for their lives.

*The Green Cockatoo* is one of Schnitzler's most skillful and effective pieces, particularly because of the tension generated through the audience's (and the gentry's) uncertainty about what is reality and what is illusion. In the end, illusion becomes bloody reality.

Carl Schorske, in his *Fin de Siècle Vienna*, describes the basic premise upon which the play is based: "Too much dedication to the life of the senses has destroyed in the upper class the power to distinguish politics from play, sexual aggression from social revolution, art from reality. Irrationality reigns supreme over the whole." In writing this piece, Schnitzler looked squarely at the problem of Austria's psyche and society, but he did so "abstractly, lightly, ironically."

## Hitting too Close to Home

Urbach describes *The Green Cockatoo* as a perfect blend of history and theater, real deception and play acting, illusion and truth, politics and pleasure seeking. He notes that none of the characters are one dimensional or interchangeable; each is a fully realized individual. And yet all completely depend on each; all are crucial to the structure of the play.

This play, which Schnitzler called "a grotesquery in one act," caused no small disturbance at its various premieres. At Vienna's Burgtheater, a Viennese archduchess insisted it be removed from the stage, which it was after only eight performances; and in Berlin, earlier, it had been banned. Paul Skrine (*Hauptmann, Wedekind and Schnitzler*) notes how the play within the play takes on a life of its own, casting doubt on the reality that surrounds it.

Henri assumes the role of a deceived husband while, in reality, his pretty wife is deceiving him with a duke. As he inveighs against the privileged and dissolute nobleman, everyone assumes he is playacting, so that, when it occurs, his murder of the duke seems so "in character" and so obviously part of the play being extemporized that it cannot be taken seriously. Where, then, does make-believe end and reality begin? Are we not all playing roles which ring true only now and then? These are the questions which this brilliant one-act play poses and which it answers strictly in terms of theatre; in doing so it brings to the surface the deepest anxieties of a society in decay and exorcises them by a dazzling exercise in dramatic irony which reaches its ultimate twist after the final curtain as we, the audience, emerge into the "real" world and have to face the fact that what we have

just witnessed was no more, and no less, than a play
conceived by Schnitzler at the height of his powers.

## *THE UNDISCOVERED COUNTRY*

Completed in 1911, *The Undiscovered Country (Das Weite Land)* went
through a lengthy gestation process that began as early as 1901.
During that ten-year period, the Austro-Hungarian Empire was
seriously on the decline and with it a way of life. *The Undiscovered
Country* addresses how people rejected the reality of that decline for
their peace of mind. A parallel in dramatic literature of the same
period is Chekhov's *The Cherry Orchard* (1904), which also deals with
the death of a way of life and its upper-class characters' refusal to
recognize the situation and their inevitable fate. The major difference
is that the theme of death in Schnitzler's work is more deeply and
psychologically rooted than it is in Chekhov.

In *The Undiscovered Country*, death enters in the first few pages.
The play opens with the funeral of Korsakov, a famous young pianist.
He has committed suicide, and this suicide is the catalyst for much of
what happens in the play. Swales, in his study of Schnitzler, notes that
death is the one certain and unavoidable event for the characters in
this play. The awareness of death makes them crave life, to desperately
grasp at experience. Fear and awareness of death also heightens
sexuality. The characters' obsession with death may be, as Swales says,
a symptom of the "doomed, decayed world" of the empire in its last
years.

### Time and Morality

Time also plays an important part in Schnitzler's view of the empire in
decline. Time is always fleeting. It's the great highway robber on the
road of life — unfair, merciless. Friedrich's duel with the twenty-four-

year-old Otto, ending in the young man's death, expresses best this sense of time passing relentlessly.

Otto has had an affair with Genia, Friedrich's wife, and Friedrich must defend his honor with a duel. But there is more to it than that. As a middle-aged man, Friedrich knows his time is near; his carefree youth is long past. To twenty-year-old Erna (with whom he is determined to have an affair), he reveals the hidden reason why he shot Otto: "I know what youth is. Not an hour past I saw it gleaming and laughing in a cold, insolent eye. I know what youth is. And I can hardly shoot them all." By shooting young Otto, Friedrich tries to maintain his own place in the stream of things. He cannot bear to see youth — insolent, proud of its strength, facing death with fearless indifference, believing itself to be immortal — because he is no longer part of it.

Morality is on a shaky foundation in Schnitzler's world and changes from day to day. Early in *The Undiscovered Country* we learn that Korsakov was hopelessly in love with Friedrich's wife, Genia, and committed suicide because she refused him in order to remain faithful to Friedrich. When Friedrich learns this, he criticizes her for her foolishness and insensitivity, for valuing something as insignificant as marital fidelity over a man's life. And yet, when Genia has an affair with Otto, Friedrich, without a moment's thought, demands satisfaction by means of a duel. At that moment, Friedrich's honor is at stake. If Genia, in Friedrich's eyes, is reprehensible for sacrificing a man's life to remain faithful to her husband, how does Friedrich justify sacrificing a man's life for the sake of his honor? He can't, of course, and he doesn't — it never occurs to him.

It is this sort of moral confusion that is a part of the sickness of Schnitzler's world. Diplomacy, understanding, and love are sidestepped for blind response. There is something morally defective here. For all the wit, grace, and charm of *The Undiscovered Country*, the endless tennis parties, the casual but hidden affairs, the veneer of high civility, it is fraught with a terrible, self-devouring duplicity.

# PROFESSOR BERNHARDI

The theme of corruption is at the very core of Schnitzler's play *Professor Bernhardi* (1912). As Swales sees it, human society is, for Schnitzler, corrupt. Worse, he can't even trust the integrity of the heart, so he concerns himself with the minds of his characters. Schnitzler is not only a perceptive and penetrating psychologist, he is, says Swales, an "astringent moralist of the heart. . . . Schnitzler's work is, in fact, a most poignant revelation of the moral bankruptcy of his times, and the dilemma in which he as a moralist finds himself is symptomatic of his position in an age where there is no common denominator to interpret and evaluate reality." Gone in his plays is the man who knows the answers (Max in *Anatol*, Theodore in *Flirtation*). No one person stands for right moral values. Morality is an interaction between attitudes and actions.

*Professor Bernhardi* opens with a girl dying at the Elizabeth Institute Hospital, founded and directed by Bernhardi. The girl, with only minutes to live, has been given a sedative to kill the pain, and it has made her euphoric. A Catholic priest is called by one of the doctors, but when he arrives, Bernhardi very gently but firmly tells the priest that he can't go to the girl's bedside because he would terrify her: She would know she was dying. From Bernhardi's point of view, it is his moral and ethical duty as the girl's doctor to give her as peaceful a death as possible.

This situation is almost immediately blown up into monstrous proportions. Bernhardi is attacked from religious, racial, and political positions. Being a Jew in a virulently anti-Semitic, turn-of-the-century Vienna, he becomes the victim of a political witch hunt. He is charged with religious agitation, prosecuted in court and sentenced, and driven out by the anti-Semitic faction in his own hospital.

Schnitzler could have easily made Bernhardi into a martyr, a morally right hero struggling against the morally wrong social collective. Instead, Schnitzler creates a much more complex and realistic situation. Rather than Bernhardi the hero, Schnitzler gives us a man who has his own set of weaknesses and blind spots. When speaking to a governmental official, he retorts scornfully: "What have I to do with politics!" To which the official responds realistically: "We all have to do with politics." At that moment, the official is the mouthpiece for Schnitzler, saying, in effect, that there is no justification for political innocence, especially in a society as divided as turn-of-the-century Vienna. Swales notes that Bernhardi, by insisting that his decision to keep the priest from the dying girl's bedside was strictly personal, fails to acknowledge that he was acting as a doctor, not a private individual, and therefore has a responsibility to the medical profession and his fellow doctors. He is incapable of acting in the public sphere, fearful of becoming involved in politics. It is to Schnitzler's credit as a playwright that the play's main character has such a limiting and fundamental weakness. Bernhardi becomes nearly an antihero. We love him for his decency, honesty, and concern for his profession — at the same realizing he is a deeply flawed man.

## FINAL YEARS

*Professor Bernhardi* is among the last works that Schnitzler wrote in the final phase of his life, from 1912 to his death in 1931. Other works he wrote during this period, often referred to as his "retrospective period," are *Beatrice* (*Frau Beate und Ihr Sohn*, 1913) and *Casanova's Homecoming* (*Casanovas Heimfahrt*, 1918). Schnitzler died of a brain hemorrhage in Vienna on October 21, 1931.

# DRAMATIC MOMENTS

## from the Major Plays

These short excerpts are from the playwright's major plays. They give a taste of the work of the playwright. Each has a short introduction in brackets that helps the reader understand the context of the excerpt. The excerpts, which are in chronological order, illustrate the main themes mentioned in the In an Hour essay.

## CHARACTERS

Max
Anatol
Cora

[*Anatol* is a series of seven one-acts united by the character of Anatol, a sophisticated young man about town. In each one-act, he is with a different mistress. In the following act, Cora, his current mistress, has agreed to be hypnotized by Anatol. Unbeknownst to Cora, Anatol wants to find out if she has other lovers. Max, Anatol's friend and adviser, is also present.]

*Anatol's Room.*

MAX: Anatol, I envy you. *(ANATOL smiles.)* I'm — I'm flabbergasted. I used to think it was nonsense. But you actually put her to sleep. She danced when you said she was a ballerina. Cried when you told her her lover was dead. And pardoned a criminal when you crowned her queen.

ANATOL: That's the way it goes.

MAX: You're a magician.

ANATOL: As are we all.

MAX: Unbelievable.

ANATOL: No more than life itself. No more than centuries of other discoveries. Think of our ancestors. When they discovered the earth turned.

MAX: But that was *every*one's concern.

ANATOL: Suppose we'd just discovered spring. Who'd believe it? Green trees and flowers not withstanding. Not to mention love.

MAX: You're being evasive. Be reasonable. But magnetism —

ANATOL: Hypnotism.

MAX: — is quite another matter. You'll never find *me* being hypnotized.

ANATOL: Don't be childish. I tell you to go to sleep. You lie down. You relax.

MAX: And suddenly I'm a chimney-sweep. Climbing up. Getting all sooty.

ANATOL: Practical jokes. What's important is its scientific application. Unfortunately we're not that far along yet.

MAX: Explain.

ANATOL: Me, for example. I put that girl into a dozen different worlds today. But can I do the same for myself?

MAX: Why not?

ANATOL: Not for lack of trying. I've stared at this diamond in my ring for minutes on end, mumbling: "Anatol, go to sleep. And when you wake, every thought of that distressing female will have vanished from your mind."

MAX: And?

ANATOL: Never got to sleep.

MAX: You're still involved with her?

ANATOL: Involved! I'm desperate! I'm insane!

MAX: Then you still have doubts?

ANATOL: Doubts? No. She deceives me right and left. When we're kissing. When she caresses my hair. When we're — Deception, deception!

MAX: You're mad.

ANATOL: Don't be a fool.

MAX: Then prove it.

ANATOL: I *sense* it! I *feel* it! *That's* how I know!

MAX: Very logical, I must say.

ANATOL: Women are unfaithful. It's their nature. And they don't even realize it. *I* read two or three books at once. *They* have two or three love affairs at once.

MAX: Does she love you?

ANATOL: Passionately! But the point is, she's unfaithful.

MAX: With whom?

ANATOL: How should I know? With a prince she met on the street. With a poet from the suburbs.

MAX: You're a fool.

ANATOL: And why not? She's like all the others. Loves life. But not a thought in her head. I ask if she loves me. She says yes. And she means it. Are you faithful? I ask. Of course, she says. And she means it. Because she's forgotten the others. At least for the moment. And what girl has ever admitted to being unfaithful? They're unfathomable! And if one *were* to admit being faithful —

MAX: Hmm?

ANATOL: — it would be pure coincidence.

MAX: But if she loves you?

ANATOL: Dear, naive Max! As if that were a reason.

MAX: Well?

ANATOL: Rather ask why am *I* unfaithful to *her*. I'm certainly in love with her.

MAX: But you're a man.

ANATOL: That old cliché. We insist on women being different from us. Well, maybe those whose mothers locked them up. Or ones with no spirit. But we're alike. If I say to a woman that I love her and only her, well, it's not really lying. Even if I did spend last night curled around someone else.

MAX: Well, of course, *you*!

ANATOL: *Me, yes*! But not *you*, I suppose. Nor my dear Cora, I suppose. It's driving me mad! What if I got down on my knees and told her that I forgive her in advance, if only she'll tell me the truth. Nonsense. She'd lie just the same. Do you suppose no girl has ever asked me if I'm being true to her? I answer, of course. But I lie. Quietly. With a sweet smile on my face. And the clearest of consciences. Why upset them? And they believe me and are happy.

MAX: So there you are.

ANATOL: But *I* don't believe it. And *I'm* not happy. Oh, I might be. If there were some way of bringing these stupid, lovable, despicable creatures to confess. Or some other way of discovering the truth. But there *is* none. None but chance.

MAX: What about hypnosis?

ANATOL: What?

MAX: Hypnosis. Put her to sleep and demand the truth.

ANATOL: Good God!

MAX: You ask her if she loves you? Is there anyone else? Where does she come from? Where is she going? What's the other fellow's name? Etcetera, etcetera, and so forth.

ANATOL: Max! Max!

MAX: Well?

ANATOL: I'd be a magician. I'd actually worm an honest word from a woman's mouth!

MAX: There you are. Salvation is in sight. Cora will make an excellent medium. By this evening you'll know whether she's faithful, or —

ANATOL: Or I'm the luckiest man alive. Max, I could kiss you. I'm free. I'm a new man. Power over a woman at last.

MAX: I'm really quite curious.

ANATOL: Oh? Do you suspect anything?

MAX: Ah, so only *you* are allowed to have doubts?

ANATOL: Of course. If a husband walks out of his house having discovered his wife in bed with her lover, and a friend comes by and says, "I suspect your wife's having an affair," the husband's not going to say, "I know; I've just seen them," but, "You, sir, are a bastard!"

MAX: Yes. I forgot. The first duty of a friend is to preserve illusion.

ANATOL: Shh!

MAX: What?

ANATOL: Footsteps in the hall. I recognized them the moment they entered downstairs.

MAX: I don't hear anything.

ANATOL: They're coming closer. They're on the stairs now. *(He opens the door.)* Cora!

CORA: *(From outside the door.)* Good evening. Oh! You have company.

ANATOL: My friend Max.

CORA: *(Entering.)* Good evening. Sitting in the dark?

ANATOL: It's dusk. You know how fond I am of this light.

CORA: *(Caressing his hair.)* My little poet.

ANATOL: Dear Cora.

CORA: Still, I think I'll light the candles. Do you mind? *(She lights the candles in the candelabra.)*

ANATOL: *(To MAX.)* Isn't she ravishing?

MAX: Ah!

CORA: What have you two been up to? Been talking long?

ANATOL: Half an hour.

CORA: Good. *(She removes her hat and coat.)* What about? Or shouldn't I ask?

ANATOL: This and that.

MAX: Hypnosis, as a matter of fact.

CORA: Oh! Not again! I'll go insane!

ANATOL: Well!

CORA: Anatol, dear. Would you hypnotize me? Sometime?

ANATOL: I? Hypnotize *you*?

CORA: I'd love it. As long as it was you.

ANATOL: Thanks.

CORA: I'd never let a stranger. Well. You know.

ANATOL: Yes, well. I'll—I'll hypnotize you.

CORA: When?

ANATOL: Now.

CORA: Wonderful. What do I do?

ANATOL: Sit quietly. Here. In this armchair. And be willing to fall asleep.

CORA: I'm willing.

ANATOL: I'll stand here in front of you. And you'll look at me. Well?

Look at me. And I'll lightly stroke your forehead. And your eyes. There.

CORA: And then?

ANATOL: That's all. You must be willing to fall asleep.

CORA: It feels so strange. You stroking my eyes like that.

ANATOL: Be still. Don't talk. Sleep. You're very tired.

CORA: No —

ANATOL: You are. Just a bit.

CORA: Yes. Just a bit.

ANATOL: Your eyelids are growing heavy. Very heavy. You can scarcely lift your hands.

CORA: *(Softly.)* Yes —

ANATOL: *(Continues to stroke her forehead and eyes; in a monotone.)* Tired. You're very tired. Go to sleep now. Sleep. *(He turns towards MAX, looking on in amazement, with a triumphant expression.)* Sleep. Your eyes are tightly closed. You can't even open them. *(CORA tries to open her eyes.)* Don't even try. You are asleep. Just sleep quietly. There.

MAX: *(Wanting to ask something.)* Anatol —

ANATOL: Shh! *(To CORA.)* Sleep. Deep, deep sleep. *(He stands for a while in front of CORA who breathes softly while she sleeps.)* There. Now you can ask your question.

MAX: Is she really asleep?

ANATOL: See for yourself. We'll wait a few moments, though. *(He stands in front of CORA and looks at her quietly. Long pause.)* Cora! You will answer me now. Answer me. What is your name?

CORA: Cora.

ANATOL: Cora, we are in the forest.

CORA: Oh, the forest! How beautiful! Green trees and — and nightingales!

ANATOL: Cora, you will tell me the truth. No matter what I ask. What will you do, Cora?

CORA: I will tell you the truth.

ANATOL: You will answer every question. Truthfully. And when you
wake up you will have forgotten everything. Do you understand?

CORA: Yes.

ANATOL: Just sleep. Sleep. *(To MAX.)* I'll ask her now.

MAX: How old is she?

ANATOL: Nineteen. Cora, how old are you?

CORA: Twenty-one.

MAX: Haha!

ANATOL: Shh! Extraordinary. Well! That only goes to show you.

MAX: Little did she know what a good subject she'd make.

ANATOL: The suggestion worked. I'll ask her another question. Cora?
Do you love me? Cora? Do you love me?

CORA: Yes.

ANATOL: *(Triumphantly.)* Did you hear?

MAX: And the big question? Is she faithful?

ANATOL: Cora! *(Turning around.)* The question is stupid.

MAX: Why?

ANATOL: I can't just ask it like that.

MAX: Aha.

ANATOL: I need to phrase it differently.

MAX: Sounds fine to me.

ANATOL: No. It's not fine at all.

MAX: Why?

ANATOL: If I asked if she were faithful to me, she might take it much
too generally.

MAX: And so?

ANATOL: She could take it to refer to her entire past. A time when she
was in love with someone else. And answer no.

MAX: That could be interesting.

ANATOL: Thanks a lot. I know that Cora knew others before me. She
said once that, had she known that one day she would meet me, she
would have —

MAX: But she *didn't* know.

ANATOL: No.

MAX: And your question?

ANATOL: Yes, the question. It's a bit clumsy. In its present form.

MAX: In that case, ask her: "Cora, have you been true to me since we met?"

ANATOL: Hmm. Not bad. *(In front of CORA.)* Cora, have you been — Oh, that's silly.

MAX: Silly?

ANATOL: Really now. You need to visualize the circumstances that brought us together. We had no idea we'd fall so desperately in love. During those first days we thought of it as a passing fancy. Who knows —

MAX: Who knows what?

ANATOL: Who knows whether she didn't start loving me just as she stopped loving someone else? And who knows what happened to her on the day we met. Before we'd even exchanged a word. Was she able to break loose from the old affair without further involvement? Or did she have to drag around those old chains for days. Even weeks.

MAX: Hmm.

ANATOL: And I'll go even further. At first it was only a whim on her part. And on mine. Neither of us saw it as anything else. All we asked of each other was a moment of sweet, fleeting happiness. If at the time she committed an indiscretion, am I to blame for it? Well. Hardly.

MAX: You're very lenient, I must say.

ANATOL: Not at all. It's just inappropriate to take advantage of the situation.

MAX: How noble. May I help extricate you from this — dilemma?

ANATOL: What?

MAX: All you need to say is: "Cora, since you've been in love with me, have you been true?"

ANATOL: That seems clear enough.

MAX: Well then.

ANATOL: But it's not.

MAX: I see.

ANATOL: Well. Just suppose that yesterday she was riding in a train compartment. And a man sitting opposite her touched the tip of her shoe with his. Now. With the characteristic heightening of perception brought on by sleep, and with the greatly sensitized condition of the medium's mind during hypnosis, it is not at all impossible for her to consider even *this* a breach of fidelity.

MAX: Great heavens!

ANATOL: All the more so since she's come to know my *own* perhaps exaggerated views on the matter. I've as much as told her: "Cora, if you even *look* at another man, you're being unfaithful to me."

MAX: And her reply?

ANATOL: She laughed. Asked how I could possibly *think* she'd even look at another man.

MAX: Yet you still think — ?

ANATOL: Accidents happen. Just suppose some arrogant man should come along some night and kiss her on the neck.

MAX: Well. Yes. Of course.

ANATOL: It's not all *that* impossible.

MAX: What you're saying is that you don't want to ask her.

ANATOL: I *do*, but —

MAX: Your objections are nonsense. When you ask a woman if she's been faithful, she knows what you're saying. Whisper tenderly in her ear: "Are you true to me?" and the man's foot or the importunate kiss would instantly flee her mind. Her understanding of infidelity is no different from yours. Which gives you the advantage of asking additional questions that will make her answers perfectly clear.

ANATOL: Then I should question her?

MAX: It's you who want to know.

ANATOL: Something else just occurred to me.

MAX: Yes?

ANATOL: The unconscious.

MAX: The unconscious?

ANATOL: I believe that there are unconscious states of mind.

MAX: And so?

ANATOL: Such states of mind arise naturally. But they may also be induced by artificial means. Means that dull or exhilarate the senses.

MAX: I'm afraid I don't —

ANATOL: Imagine a mysterious, twilit room.

MAX: Twilit. Mysterious. Yes. I'm imagining.

ANATOL: And in that room — there is she — and another —

MAX: How did she get there?

ANATOL: We'll come back to that. There are ways. In any case, it *could* happen. And then — a couple of glasses of Rhine wine. A certain heaviness in the air that seems to weigh on everything. The fragrance of cigarettes. Perfumed wallpaper. The dim light of frosted chandeliers reflecting red silk curtains. Solitude. Silence. The whisper of tender words —

MAX: Aha —

ANATOL: Others have been had in such circumstances. Better ones than she. More placid than she —

MAX: How do I reconcile fidelity and her being in that scene with another man?

ANATOL: Life has its enigmas.

MAX: Anatol! You have the opportunity to resolve the enigma that the world's wisest men have beaten their heads over! If only you'd ask the question. *One question* will tell you whether you are among the few who are loved exclusively by one woman; the identity of your rival in love; and by what means he succeeded. And yet you refuse! You have the power to question fate! But you *won't*! The truth is at your fingertips! And you do nothing! Do you know why? Because the woman you love is the same as you suppose all women to be. And because illusion is a thousand times more dear to you than the truth. Let's stop this. Wake her up, and be satisfied that — that you might have accomplished a miracle.

ANATOL: Max!

MAX: Am I wrong? Your words are empty phrases, Anatol, that deceived neither of us. That's what all this has been about.

ANATOL: *(Quickly.)* But, Max. I *do* want to ask her. I *will* ask her.

MAX: Aha.

ANATOL: Don't be angry with me, Max. Just not with you in the room.

MAX: What?

ANATOL: When she tells me she's been unfaithful, I want to be the only one to hear it. Unhappiness is only half of the misfortune. Being pitied for it is *total* misery. I couldn't bear that. You're my best friend. I don't want your pity telling me how miserable I am. Maybe I'm just ashamed in front of you. You'll know the truth in any case. If it's true, you'll never see her again. I just want to hear it by myself.

MAX: Of course. *(He shakes ANATOL's hand.)* I'll go.

ANATOL: Dear Max. *(He accompanies MAX to the door.)* I won't be more than a minute. *(MAX goes out. ANATOL stands in front of CORA, looking at her for a long while.)* Cora! *(Shakes his head and walks about.)* Cora! *(Kneels in front of her.)* Cora! My sweet Cora! — Cora! *(He rises; with resolution.)* Wake up! Kiss me!

CORA: *(Rises, rubs her eyes and throws her arms around ANATOL's neck.)* Anatol! Was I asleep long? Where's Max?

ANATOL: Max!

MAX: *(Entering from the adjoining room.)* Here I am.

ANATOL: Yes, quite a while. And you talked in your sleep.

CORA: Oh, I didn't! Anything interesting?

MAX: You answered the questions he put to you.

CORA: What did he ask?

ANATOL: All sorts of things.

CORA: And I answered them?

ANATOL: Every one.

CORA: Well, what did you ask?

ANATOL: None of your business. Tomorrow I'll hypnotize you again.

CORA: Oh, no. Not me. It's witchcraft. You wake up and don't know what you've said. All I know is I talked a lot of nonsense.

ANATOL: For example. That you love me.

CORA: Oh?

MAX: Doesn't believe it herself. Too much!

CORA: I didn't need to be asleep to tell you that.

ANATOL: My angel!

*(They embrace.)*

MAX: Dear friends, I bid you good night.

ANATOL: Going? So soon?

MAX: I must.

ANATOL: Forgive me if I don't show you out.

CORA: See you.

MAX: My pleasure. *(At the door.)* I've learned one thing for certain. That women are capable of lying even under hypnosis. But they're happy. And that's all that matters. Goodbye, my dears.

*(They fail to hear MAX because they are entwined in a passionate embrace.)*

## (END OF THE SCENE)
****

## from **ANATOL**
### from *Christmas Shopping* (1891)

## CHARACTERS

Anatol

Gabrielle

[In this one-act from the Anatol series, Anatol runs into Gabrielle, an upper-class married woman. Anatol was and still is interested in Gabrielle, but she has refused to have an affair with him.]

*It is six o'clock on a Christmas Eve in the streets of Vienna. Light snowfall.*

ANATOL: Madam? Madam?

GABRIELLE: I beg your — ? Oh! It's you!

ANATOL: Yes. I'm following you. I can't bear to have you carry all those things. Here. Give me those packages.

GABRIELLE: No, no. Thank you. I can manage.

ANATOL: Why are you making it so difficult? All I want is to be gallant for a change.

GABRIELLE: Well. Perhaps this one.

ANATOL: This? Oh, come now. Give them to me. There. And that one. And that one there.

GABRIELLE: That's quite enough. Really. You're much too kind.

ANATOL: And you're kind for letting me help. It happens far too seldom.

GABRIELLE: In your case only in the street. And when it's snowing.

ANATOL: And night coming on. And just by chance Christmas Eve.

GABRIELLE: I can't believe it's you.

ANATOL: What you mean is, I haven't called on you all season.

GABRIELLE: Yes. Something like that.

ANATOL: My dear lady. I'm not making calls this season. None. And how is your husband? And the children?

GABRIELLE: Why not spare yourself all this? You're not the least bit interested.

ANATOL: How perceptive. Uncanny.

GABRIELLE: I know you.

ANATOL: Not as well as I could wish.

GABRIELLE: I could do without your observations.

ANATOL: But I can't help myself.

GABRIELLE: Please. My packages.

ANATOL: No, don't be angry. Please. I'll behave. *(They walk along in silence.)*

GABRIELLE: You can *talk*, you know. I didn't mean *that*.

ANATOL: Yes. Well. When madam commands —

GABRIELLE: Entertain me. It's been so long. What have you been up to?

ANATOL: Nothing. As usual.

GABRIELLE: Nothing?

ANATOL: Not a thing.

GABRIELLE: Pity!

ANATOL: And you couldn't care less.

GABRIELLE: You know that, do you?

ANATOL: Loafing my life away. And whose fault is that? Whose?

GABRIELLE: The packages. Please.

ANATOL: It was only a question.

GABRIELLE: Do you walk often?

ANATOL: "Walk"? You ask that with such contempt. It's a marvelous pastime. Such an aimless word. Unfortunately today I'm not aimless. Today I'm busy. As you are, dear lady.

GABRIELLE: Oh?

ANATOL: Buying Christmas presents. Like you.

GABRIELLE: You?

ANATOL: But nothing suits me. Evening after evening I've pored over Vienna's shop windows. Up one street. Down another. There's not a tasteful or imaginative item to be had.

GABRIELLE: That's for the buyer to supply. You should invent for yourself. You certainly have the time. And order your presents during the autumn.

ANATOL: Not my style, I'm afraid. How am I to know in autumn who I'll give presents to at Christmas? No thanks. So here I am again. Two hours before candle-lighting. And still no idea. Not a one.

GABRIELLE: May I help?

ANATOL: You're an angel. Just leave me with the packages. All right?

GABRIELLE: No.

ANATOL: Ah! Then I *can* call you angel. Nice. Angel!

GABRIELLE: Just be quiet.

ANATOL: I'll sit on my tongue.

GABRIELLE: Give me some hints. Who's the gift for?

ANATOL: That's a difficult one.

GABRIELLE: A lady? Of course.

ANATOL: Yes. As a matter of fact. You're very perceptive. Once again.

GABRIELLE: Exactly what *sort* of lady? A *real* one?

ANATOL: Depends on how you define your terms. If by *lady* you mean a woman of the great world, then the definition falls short.

GABRIELLE: The small world then?

ANATOL: You might say that.

GABRIELLE: What else?

ANATOL: You're being catty.

GABRIELLE: I know your taste. Thin and blonde. The other side of the tracks.

ANATOL: Blonde? Yes. I must admit.

GABRIELLE: Blonde it is. You're very consistent. All those girls from the suburbs.

ANATOL: Is that my fault? My dear?

GABRIELLE: Shall we drop the subject? I like people who stick with their kind. Imagine forsaking the scene of your triumphs.

ANATOL: I have no choice. I'm loved only in the suburbs.

GABRIELLE: And do they *understand* you? In the suburbs?

ANATOL: Not at all. I'm loved in the suburbs. In the great world I'm only understood. You know how it is.

GABRIELLE: I'm afraid I don't. Nor do I care to. Ah! Here we are! Just the shop we're looking for. Your little miss shall have a lovely present.

ANATOL: You're too kind.

GABRIELLE: Why, look here. A fancy little box with three different perfumes. Or this! With six cakes of soap. Patchouli. Chypre. Jockey Club. That should be just the thing.

ANATOL: You're very cruel, my dear.

GABRIELLE: No, no. Look here. A small brooch with six paste diamonds. Just imagine! Six! And how it glitters! Or this bracelet. With the divine trinkets dangling from it. One the head of a moor. That should go down well. In the suburbs.

ANATOL: You're quite wrong, I'm afraid — dear lady. You don't understand this sort of girl. They're quite different from what you imagine.

GABRIELLE: And there! Oh, how charming! Come closer. Well? What do you think of the hat? Three years ago the style was an absolute rage. The sweeping feathers! What do you think? This will be a sensation in the provinces!

ANATOL: I don't believe we were discussing the provinces, madam. And besides, you underestimate the taste even of the provinces.

GABRIELLE: Yes. Well. You're not being very helpful. Any suggestions?

ANATOL: How can I? Your answer would be a condescending smile.

GABRIELLE: Listen to you! I want to learn about her. Is she vain? Is she modest? Is she large? Is she small? Does she like bright colors — ?

ANATOL: I should never have accepted your kind offer. You're mocking me.

GABRIELLE: But I'm all ears. Tell me about her.

ANATOL: I don't dare.

GABRIELLE: Don't dare? Since when?

ANATOL: Shall we change the subject?

GABRIELLE: No. But I insist. How long have you known her?

ANATOL: For some time.

GABRIELLE: Must I drag it out by the tail? Tell me.

ANATOL: There's nothing to tell.

GABRIELLE: Where, how, when you met her. What sort of person she is. Well?

ANATOL: Fine. But you may find it boring. I've warned you.

GABRIELLE: I won't be bored. I want to learn about that world. What's it like? I'm really quite ignorant.

ANATOL: You wouldn't understand.

GABRIELLE: You're off again.

ANATOL: You have contempt for everything outside your little circle. And you're very wrong.

GABRIELLE: I can be taught. No one ever tells me anything. How can I be expected to —

ANATOL: And yet you're always afraid of losing something if you go too far. A kind of silent enmity.

GABRIELLE: No one takes from me what I don't want to lose.

ANATOL: You may not want it. Yet you don't want anyone else having it.

GABRIELLE: Oh!

ANATOL: That, my dear, is being feminine. And being feminine, it's very noble and beautiful and profound.

GABRIELLE: Where do you come by your irony.

ANATOL: I'll tell you. I, too, was innocent once. Full of trust. Without scorn. And I suffered my wounds silently.

GABRIELLE: Don't romanticize.

ANATOL: Honest wounds, that is. I could endure a No spoken at the right time. Even from lips I loved dearly. But a No when the eyes have said Perhaps a hundred times over — when the lips have smiled Maybe a hundred times over — when the tone of voice sounded Yes a hundred times over — such a No is enough to —

GABRIELLE: We were buying a present.

ANATOL: Such a No makes a man either a fool or a cynic.

GABRIELLE: You were going to — tell me —

ANATOL: Very well. If you insist.

GABRIELLE: Of course I insist. How did you meet her?

ANATOL: Good God! The same way one meets anyone. In the street. At a dance. On a bus. Under an umbrella —

GABRIELLE: Yes. Of course. But — it's this particular case I'm interested in. We were to buy a present for this particular case. Remember?

ANATOL: Over there — in that "small world" — there *are* no particular cases. No more than in the "great world." You're all so true to type.

GABRIELLE: Sir, you're beginning to —

ANATOL: That's no insult. Not at all. I'm true to type myself.

GABRIELLE: What type?

ANATOL: Frivolous melancholic.

GABRIELLE: And? And I?

ANATOL: You? Easy. Lady of fashion.

GABRIELLE: I see. And she?

ANATOL: She? She is — the sweet young thing.

GABRIELLE: Sweet. Did you say sweet? Then that leaves me simply a — a lady of fashion.

ANATOL: A wicked lady of fashion, if you insist.

GABRIELLE: Well. Do tell me about this — sweet young thing.

ANATOL: She's not fascinatingly beautiful. She's not particularly elegant. And she's certainly not bright.

GABRIELLE: I'm not interested in what she's *not*.

ANATOL: But she has the gentle charm of a spring evening. The grace of an enchanted princess. The spirit of a girl who knows how to love.

GABRIELLE: The kind of spirit that is rather commonplace in your "small world."

ANATOL: There's no way you could understand. As a young girl you were told too little. And as a young woman too much. Consequently you're rather naive.

GABRIELLE: But I've already told you. I want to learn. I'm willing to believe in your "enchanted princess." But do tell me about the magic garden she reclines in.

ANATOL: Well. You mustn't imagine a glittering drawing room with heavy curtains and pale velvets. Nor the affected twilight of a dying afternoon.

GABRIELLE: Please don't tell me what I *mustn't* imagine.

ANATOL: Fine! Then imagine a small — a very small, dim room with painted walls. Somewhat too light in tone. A few dreadful engravings with faded lettering hanging here and there. And a lamp with a shade. From the window at evening you have a view of roofs and chimneys receding into the dusk. And — when spring comes, the garden opposite will burst into blossom and send out its fragrance.

GABRIELLE: How happy to think of May on Christmas Eve.

ANATOL: Yes. I'm happy there occasionally.

GABRIELLE: But enough of this. It's getting late. And we were buying her something. Something for the room with the painted walls?

ANATOL: It has all it needs.

GABRIELLE: For *her* taste, yes. But I'd like to decorate the room to — to suit *your* taste.

ANATOL: *My* taste!

GABRIELLE: With Persian carpets —

ANATOL: In the suburbs! Really!

GABRIELLE: — and a red and green cut-glass lamp.

ANATOL: Hm.

GABRIELLE: And vases of fresh flowers.

ANATOL: But I wanted something for *her*.

GABRIELLE: Yes. Of course. How silly of me. Decisions, decisions! I suppose she's waiting for you? This very moment?

ANATOL: I'm sure.

GABRIELLE: Is she really?! But tell me. How does she welcome you?

ANATOL: Oh — the usual way, I suppose.

GABRIELLE: Listens for your footsteps on the stairs? Hm?

ANATOL: Sometimes. Yes.

GABRIELLE: And waits by the door?

ANATOL: Yes!

GABRIELLE: And then falls into your arms. Kisses you. And says — . Tell me what she says.

ANATOL: What one usually says.

GABRIELLE: For example.

ANATOL: I can't think of one.

GABRIELLE: Well. Yesterday.

ANATOL: Oh — nothing in particular. It sounds stupid without the sound of her voice.

GABRIELLE: In that case I'll imagine it. I'm waiting. What did she say?

ANATOL: "I'm so happy to have you again."

GABRIELLE: "I'm so happy" — . What was it?

ANATOL: — "to have you again."

GABRIELLE: That's quite sweet. Really. Quite sweet.

ANATOL: Yes. It's sincere.

GABRIELLE: And she's — alone, is she? You can see each other without being — disturbed?

ANATOL: Yes. She's independent. No father. No mother. Not even an aunt.

GABRIELLE: And you — are her everything?

ANATOL: I suppose. Today.

GABRIELLE: It's getting late. The streets are empty.

ANATOL: I'm sorry. I've kept you. You should be home by now.

GABRIELLE: Yes. I should. They're waiting for me. But what shall we do about the present?

ANATOL: Oh — I'll pick up something or other.

GABRIELLE: You never know. Still, I did say I'd choose something for your — for the — girl.

ANATOL: Don't bother. Please.

GABRIELLE: I wish so much I could be there when you give her her Christmas present. To see her tiny room and — and the sweet young thing. She has no idea how lucky she is.

ANATOL: — ?

GABRIELLE: I can take my parcels now. It's quite late —

ANATOL: Certainly. Here you are. But —

GABRIELLE: Could you hail that cab?

ANATOL: Why the rush all of a sudden?

GABRIELLE: Please. Please. *(He motions for the cab.)* Thank you very much. Oh, but the present. *(The cab has stopped beside them. ANATOL starts to open the door.)* Wait. I'd like to send her something myself.

ANATOL: You?! But, my dear lady!

GABRIELLE: Why shouldn't I? Take these. These flowers. Just these flowers. It's only a greeting. Nothing more. But you must promise to give her a message with them.

ANATOL: You're very kind.

GABRIELLE: Promise you'll tell her — in these exact words —

ANATOL: Of course.

GABRIELLE: Promise?

ANATOL: My pleasure. Why not?

GABRIELLE: *(Has opened the cab door.)* Tell her —

ANATOL: Yes — ?

GABRIELLE: Tell her: "These flowers, my — sweet young thing, are a gift from a woman who might have loved as much as you — but who hadn't the courage."

ANATOL: Dear — lady!

*(She has climbed into the cab and it moves off. The streets are nearly deserted. He looks in the direction of the cab until it turns a far corner — stands there for a while, looks at his watch and hurries away.)*

(END OF THE SCENE)

****

# from **La Ronde** (1897–99)

## CHARACTERS

Young Gentleman
Young Wife

[*La Ronde* is a series of ten scenes. In each, a man and a woman meet and talk, the meeting eventually leading to sexual intercourse. The ten scenes cover the entire range of Viennese society, beginning with the lowest in Scene One (the Prostitute and the Soldier) and ending with the highest in Scene Ten (the Count). In each successive scene, the person representing the higher class reappears; thus in Scene Two, the Soldier meets the Parlor Maid. The following scene is the fourth in the sequence.]

### THE YOUNG GENTLEMAN AND THE YOUNG WIFE

*Evening. A salon in a house in Schwindgasse, furnished with cheap elegance. The YOUNG GENTLEMAN has just entered, and, while still wearing his topcoat and with hat still in hand, lights the candles. He then opens the door to the adjoining room and looks in. The light from the candles in the salon falls across the inlaid floor to the four-poster against the back wall. The reddish glow from a fireplace in the corner of the room diffuses itself on the curtains of the bed. The YOUNG GENTLEMAN also inspects the bedroom. He removes an atomizer from the dressing-table and sprays the pillows on the bed with a fine mist of violet perfume. Then he goes through both rooms with the atomizer, pressing continuously on the little bulb, until both rooms smell of violet. He removes his topcoat and hat, sits in a blue velvet armchair, and smokes. After a short while, he rises again, and assures himself that the green shutters are lowered. Suddenly he returns to the bedroom and opens the drawer of the night-table. He feels around in it for a tortoise-shell hairpin. He looks for a place to hide it, then puts it in the pocket of his topcoat. He then opens a cabinet in the salon, removes a tray with a bottle of cognac on it and two small liqueur glasses*

*which he places on the table. He goes to his topcoat and removes a small*
*white package from the pocket. Opening it, he places it beside the cognac.*
*Returns to the cabinet, and removes two small plates and eating utensils.*
*From the package he takes a marron glacé and eats it. He then pours him-*
*self a glass of cognac and drinks it. He looks at his watch. He paces the*
*room several times. He stops in front of the large mirror and combs his*
*hair and small mustache with a pocket comb. Now he goes to the door lead-*
*ing to the hallway and listens. Not a sound. The bell rings. The YOUNG*
*GENTLEMAN starts suddenly. He then sits in the armchair and rises*
*only when the door is opened and the YOUNG WIFE enters. She is heav-*
*ily veiled. Closing the door behind her, she remains standing there for a mo-*
*ment while she brings her left hand to her heart as though to master an*
*overwhelming emotion. The YOUNG GENTLEMAN goes to her, takes*
*her left hand in his and imprints a kiss on her white black-trimmed glove.*

YOUNG GENTLEMAN: *(Softly)*: Thank you.

YOUNG WIFE: Alfred! Alfred!

YOUNG GENTLEMAN: Come in, dear lady. Come in, my dear, dear
    Emma!

YOUNG WIFE: Please leave me here a while! Please, Alfred! *(She re-*
    *mains standing at the door. The YOUNG GENTLEMAN stands in front*
    *of her holding her hand.)* Where am I?

YOUNG GENTLEMAN: With me.

YOUNG WIFE: This is a frightful house, Alfred!

YOUNG GENTLEMAN: Why? It's a distinguished house.

YOUNG WIFE: I passed two gentlemen on the stairs!

YOUNG GENTLEMAN: Did you recognize them?

YOUNG WIFE: I don't know. It's possible.

YOUNG GENTLEMAN: Wouldn't you recognize your own friends?

YOUNG WIFE: I couldn't see!

YOUNG GENTLEMAN: Your best friends wouldn't have recognized
    you in that veil. Not even me.

YOUNG WIFE: Two veils!

YOUNG GENTLEMAN: Do come in. And at least take off your hat.

YOUNG WIFE: Oh, I couldn't possibly! When I agreed to come, I said
    five minutes. Not a moment longer.

YOUNG GENTLEMAN: Then your veil.

YOUNG WIFE: Two veils.

YOUNG GENTLEMAN: Both veils, then. But at least let me see you.

YOUNG WIFE: Do you love me, Alfred?

YOUNG GENTLEMAN: *(Deeply hurt.)* Emma, how *can* you.

YOUNG WIFE: It's terribly warm in here.

YOUNG GENTLEMAN: It's your fur cape. You'll catch cold if you —

YOUNG WIFE: *(Finally enters the room and throws herself into the armchair.)* I'm exhausted.

YOUNG GENTLEMAN: May I?

*(He removes her veils, takes the pin out of her hat, and places the hat, the pin, and the veils to one side. The YOUNG WIFE does not hinder him. The YOUNG GENTLEMAN stands in front of her and shakes his head.)*

YOUNG WIFE: What — ?

YOUNG GENTLEMAN: You're lovely.

YOUNG WIFE: I don't —

YOUNG GENTLEMAN: Just being alone with you. Emma. *(He kneels beside the armchair, takes her hands in his and covers them with kisses.)*

YOUNG WIFE: No. I have to go. You've had your wish. *(The YOUNG GENTLEMAN lets his head sink into her lap.)* You promised you'd behave.

YOUNG GENTLEMAN: Yes.

YOUNG WIFE: I'm about to suffocate.

YOUNG GENTLEMAN: *(Rises)* It's your fur cape.

YOUNG WIFE: Put it next to my hat.

YOUNG GENTLEMAN: *(Takes off her fur cape and places it beside the other things on the divan.)* There.

YOUNG WIFE: And now — goodbye.

YOUNG GENTLEMAN: Emma! Emma!

YOUNG WIFE: You've had your five minutes.

YOUNG GENTLEMAN: But I haven't!

YOUNG WIFE: I want to know the time, Alfred.

YOUNG GENTLEMAN: A quarter to seven exactly.

YOUNG WIFE: I should be at my sister's!

YOUNG GENTLEMAN: Your sister sees you all the time.

YOUNG WIFE: Why did you bring me here!

YOUNG GENTLEMAN: Because I worship you, Emma.

YOUNG WIFE: And I'm the first, I suppose?

YOUNG GENTLEMAN: You are now.

YOUNG WIFE: I can't believe what I've become. A week ago — even yesterday. I wouldn't have thought it possible.

YOUNG GENTLEMAN: The day before yesterday you agreed.

YOUNG WIFE: You tormented me into it. I didn't want to. God knows I didn't. I swore yesterday that — . Yesterday evening I wrote you a long letter.

YOUNG GENTLEMAN: It never arrived!

YOUNG WIFE: I destroyed it. Oh, I should have sent it!

YOUNG GENTLEMAN: It's better this way.

YOUNG WIFE: No, it's disgraceful of me. I just don't understand myself. Alfred, let me go now. Goodbye. *(The YOUNG GENTLEMAN embraces her and covers her face with passionate kisses.)* Is this how you — keep your promise?

YOUNG GENTLEMAN: Just one more kiss. Just one.

YOUNG WIFE: And the last. *(He kisses her; she returns the kiss; their lips remain locked together for a long while.)*

YOUNG GENTLEMAN: Emma! This is the first time I've ever known happiness! *(The YOUNG WIFE sinks back into the armchair. The YOUNG GENTLEMAN sits on the arm of the chair, placing his arm lightly around her neck.)* Or rather, I — know what happiness *could* be.

YOUNG WIFE: *(Sighs deeply; the YOUNG GENTLEMAN kisses her again.)* Oh, Alfred, I don't like what you've made of me.

YOUNG GENTLEMAN: Are you uncomfortable? We're safe. Better than meeting outside.

YOUNG WIFE: Don't remind me of it.

YOUNG GENTLEMAN: Those were wonderful times. I'll remember them. Every moment with you is precious.

YOUNG WIFE: Do you remember the Industrial Ball?

YOUNG GENTLEMAN: Remember?! I sat beside you during supper. Close beside. Your husband ordered champagne. *(The YOUNG WIFE looks at him in protest.)* I was only going to mention the champagne. A glass of cognac?

YOUNG WIFE: A drop. With a glass of water first.

YOUNG GENTLEMAN: Hm! Now, where is the — ah! *(He pushes aside the curtains and enters the bedroom. He then returns with a decanter of water and two drinking glasses.)*

YOUNG WIFE: Where did you go?

YOUNG GENTLEMAN: The — the next room. *(Pours a glass of water.)*

YOUNG WIFE: Now, Alfred, I — I want you to tell me the truth.

YOUNG GENTLEMAN: Promise.

YOUNG WIFE: Have there been other women here?

YOUNG GENTLEMAN: But this house is twenty years old.

YOUNG WIFE: You know what I mean. With you. Here. With you.

YOUNG GENTLEMAN: With me?! Here?! Emma! How can you — !

YOUNG WIFE: Then you — No, I'd rather not ask. I'm to blame. Nothing goes unavenged.

YOUNG GENTLEMAN: What? I don't understand. What doesn't go unavenged?

YOUNG WIFE: No, no, no, I must come to my senses! Or I'll die of shame!

YOUNG GENTLEMAN: *(Holding a water decanter, shakes his head slowly.)* Emma, how can you hurt me like this! *(The YOUNG WIFE pours herself a glass of cognac.)* I have something to say, Emma. If you're ashamed to be here, if I mean nothing to you, if you don't know that you're everything in the world to me — then — you should leave.

YOUNG WIFE: Thank you, I will.

YOUNG GENTLEMAN: *(Taking her by the hand.)* But if you know that I can't live without you, that to kiss your hand means more than all the women in the world! Emma, I'm not like those other young men who know how to court women. Maybe I'm too naive. I —

YOUNG WIFE: Suppose you *were* like all those other young men?

YOUNG GENTLEMAN: Then you wouldn't be here. Because you're not like other women.

YOUNG WIFE: Are you so sure?

YOUNG GENTLEMAN: *(Has pulled her to the divan and sat down beside her.)* I've thought about you a lot. I know you're unhappy. *(The YOUNG WIFE is pleased.)* Life is so empty, so futile! And then — so short! So terribly short. There's only one happiness. Finding someone who loves you. *(The YOUNG WIFE has taken a candied pear from the table and puts it in her mouth.)* Give me half.

YOUNG WIFE: *(Offers it to him with her lips, then takes hold of his hands threatening to go astray.)* What are you doing, Alfred? Is this keeping your promise?

YOUNG GENTLEMAN: *(Swallowing the pear; then more boldly.)* Life is so short —

YOUNG WIFE: *(Weakly.)* But there's no reason to —

YOUNG GENTLEMAN: *(Mechanically.)* Oh, but there is —

YOUNG WIFE: *(More weakly.)* Alfred, you promised to behave. And it's so light.

YOUNG GENTLEMAN: Come, my dear, my only. *(He lifts her from the divan.)*

YOUNG WIFE: What are you — ?

YOUNG GENTLEMAN: It's dark in there.

YOUNG WIFE: Another room? Alfred?

YOUNG GENTLEMAN: *(Takes her with him.)* A beautiful room — and very dark —

YOUNG WIFE: I want to stay here. *(The YOUNG GENTLEMAN is already through the curtains with her, into the bedroom, and begins to unbutton her blouse.)* You're so — oh, God, what are you — ! Alfred!

YOUNG GENTLEMAN: I worship you, Emma!

YOUNG WIFE: Please wait! Wait! *(Weakly.)* Go on. I'll call you.

YOUNG GENTLEMAN: Please. Let me — let me — let me help you —

YOUNG WIFE: You're tearing my clothes.

YOUNG GENTLEMAN: You're not wearing a corset!

YOUNG WIFE: *No!* And neither does Duse! You can unbutton my shoes. *(The YOUNG GENTLEMAN unbuttons her shoes and kisses her feet. The YOUNG WIFE has slipped into bed.)* Oh, it's cold!

YOUNG GENTLEMAN: Not for long!

YOUNG WIFE: *(Laughing softly.)* Oh?

YOUNG GENTLEMAN: *(Suddenly in a bad mood; to himself.)* Why did she say that! *(He undresses in the dark.)*

YOUNG WIFE: *(Tenderly.)* Come — come — come —

YOUNG GENTLEMAN: *(Suddenly in a better mood.)* In a second.

YOUNG WIFE: I smell violets.

YOUNG GENTLEMAN: No. *You* smell like violets. Yes. *(To her.)* You!

YOUNG WIFE: Alfred! Alfred!

****

YOUNG GENTLEMAN: I just love you too much, that's all! I feel like I'm going insane!

YOUNG WIFE: —

YOUNG GENTLEMAN: I've felt that way recently. I knew it would happen!

YOUNG WIFE: Don't be upset.

YOUNG GENTLEMAN: No. It's only natural for a man to —

YOUNG WIFE: There now. There. You're all excited. Calm down.

YOUNG GENTLEMAN: Do you know Stendhal?

YOUNG WIFE: Stendhal?

YOUNG GENTLEMAN: His *Psychology of Love.*

YOUNG WIFE: Why?

YOUNG GENTLEMAN: There's a story in it. Very significant.

YOUNG WIFE: Tell me about it.

YOUNG GENTLEMAN: Well, there's a large group of cavalry officers that's gotten together.

YOUNG WIFE: And?

YOUNG GENTLEMAN: And they tell about their love affairs. And each reports that with the woman he loves most — most passionately — Well. The same thing happened to them that just happened to us.

YOUNG WIFE: Yes —

YOUNG GENTLEMAN: There's more. One of them claims that it *never* happened to him. But Stendhal adds that he was a notorious braggart.

YOUNG WIFE: Aha.

YOUNG GENTLEMAN: But it's still a shock. Even if it doesn't mean anything. Stupid.

YOUNG WIFE: Yes, and you did promise you'd behave.

YOUNG GENTLEMAN: You're laughing! You don't know — !

YOUNG WIFE: I'm not. That bit about Stendhal was very interesting. I only thought it happened to older men. Who — who've lived a good deal.

YOUNG GENTLEMAN: That's got nothing to do with it. Besides, I didn't tell you the best story. One of the cavalry officers tells how he spent three nights — or was it six? — with a woman he'd wanted for weeks. And all they did was cry with happiness. Both of them.

YOUNG WIFE: Both of them?

YOUNG GENTLEMAN: Yes! Amazing! It makes so much sense. When you're in love.

YOUNG WIFE: But there must be many who don't cry.

YOUNG GENTLEMAN: *(Nervous.)* Well, of course. That was an exception.

YOUNG WIFE: Ah! I thought Stendhal said that *all* cavalry officers cry. Under the circumstances.

YOUNG GENTLEMAN: You're making fun of me!

YOUNG WIFE: Alfred! Don't be childish!

YOUNG GENTLEMAN: I'm nervous! And — and — it's all you're thinking about! I'm ashamed!

YOUNG WIFE: It never occurred to me.

YOUNG GENTLEMAN: You're lying! I'm not even sure you love me!

YOUNG WIFE: What else can I do?

YOUNG GENTLEMAN: You always make fun of me!

YOUNG WIFE: How silly. Come. Let me kiss that sweet face.

YOUNG GENTLEMAN: I like that.

YOUNG WIFE: Do you love me?

YOUNG GENTLEMAN: I'm *so* happy!

YOUNG WIFE: But you don't have to cry, too.

YOUNG GENTLEMAN: *(Pulling away from her; agitated.)* There. You see? And I even begged you.

YOUNG WIFE: All I said was you shouldn't cry.

YOUNG GENTLEMAN: You said: "You don't have to cry, *too*"!

YOUNG WIFE: Sweetheart, you're nervous.

YOUNG GENTLEMAN: I know!

YOUNG WIFE: But why? I love the idea that — well, that we're friends.

YOUNG GENTLEMAN: There you go again!

YOUNG WIFE: That was one of our first talks. We wanted to be good friends. Just friends. What a lovely time. It was at my sister's. The big ball in January. During the quadrille. Oh, God, I should be at my sister's now! What will she say? Goodbye, Alfred!

YOUNG GENTLEMAN: Emma! You can't leave me! Like *this*!

YOUNG WIFE: But I can.

YOUNG GENTLEMAN: Just five more minutes.

YOUNG WIFE: All right. Just five more minutes. But promise me not to move. Agreed? I'll give you a kiss when I leave. Shh! Quiet. Don't move. Or I'll leave at once, my sweet — sweet —

YOUNG GENTLEMAN: Emma! My dear, dear —

\*\*\*\*

YOUNG WIFE: Dear Alfred.

YOUNG GENTLEMAN: You're heavenly! Heavenly!

YOUNG WIFE: I have to go now.

YOUNG GENTLEMAN: Your sister can wait.

YOUNG WIFE: No! Home! It's too late for my sister's. What time is it?

YOUNG GENTLEMAN: *(Dumbfounded.)* Well, I don't know!

YOUNG WIFE: Try your watch.

YOUNG GENTLEMAN: It's in my waistcoat.

YOUNG WIFE: Then get it.

YOUNG GENTLEMAN: *(Gets out of bed with a mighty push.)* Eight.

YOUNG WIFE: *(Rises quickly.)* Oh, God! Hurry, Alfred! My stockings! What will I tell him? They're waiting for me at home! Eight o'clock!

YOUNG GENTLEMAN: When will I see you again?

YOUNG WIFE: Never.

YOUNG GENTLEMAN: Emma! You don't love me!

YOUNG WIFE: Of course I love you. Hand me my shoes.

YOUNG GENTLEMAN: But *never*? *(Hands her the shoes.)* Here.

YOUNG WIFE: There's a button-hook in my bag. Hurry! Please!

YOUNG GENTLEMAN: *(Hands her the button-hook.)* Here.

YOUNG WIFE: Alfred, this situation could become serious.

YOUNG GENTLEMAN: *(Disagreeable.)* Why?

YOUNG WIFE: What will I tell my husband? And he'll ask!

YOUNG GENTLEMAN: You've been at your sister's.

YOUNG WIFE: I can't lie. I never could.

YOUNG GENTLEMAN: There's no other way.

YOUNG WIFE: If only you were worth it. Oh, come here. I want to kiss you again. *(She embraces him.)* And now — leave me alone. Go in the other room. I can't dress with you here. *(The YOUNG GENTLEMAN goes into the salon and dresses. He eats some of the pastry and drinks a glass of cognac. The YOUNG WIFE calls after a while.)* Alfred?

YOUNG GENTLEMAN: My dear?

YOUNG WIFE: I'm glad we didn't cry.

YOUNG GENTLEMAN: *(Smiling not without pride.)* Oh! Women!

YOUNG WIFE: What will happen — if by chance we meet one day at a party?

YOUNG GENTLEMAN: By chance? One day? But you'll be at Lobheimer's tomorrow.

YOUNG WIFE: Yes. You?

YOUNG GENTLEMAN: Yes. May I have the cotillion?

YOUNG WIFE: Oh, I *can't* go! You're mad! I'd — *(she enters the salon, fully dressed, and takes a chocolate pastry)* — I'd die of embarrassment!

YOUNG GENTLEMAN: Tomorrow at Lobheimer's. It will be lovely.

YOUNG WIFE: No! I'll excuse myself! I'll —

YOUNG GENTLEMAN: Then the day after tomorrow. Here.

YOUNG WIFE: You're joking.

YOUNG GENTLEMAN: At six.

YOUNG WIFE: Are there any cabs at the corner?

YOUNG GENTLEMAN: As many as you like. The day after tomorrow. At six. Here. Say yes, my dear, my sweet.

YOUNG WIFE: We'll discuss it tomorrow. During the cotillion.

YOUNG GENTLEMAN: *(Embraces her.)* Angel!

YOUNG WIFE: Don't muss my hair.

YOUNG GENTLEMAN: Tomorrow at Lobheimer's. And the day after tomorrow here. In my arms.

YOUNG WIFE: Goodbye.

YOUNG GENTLEMAN: *(Suddenly troubled again.)* What will you tell your husband?

YOUNG WIFE: Don't ask! Don't ask! I can't bear to think! Why do I love you so? Goodbye! If I meet anyone on the stairs, I'll have a stroke! Ah!

*(The YOUNG GENTLEMAN kisses her hand once again. The YOUNG WIFE goes off. The YOUNG GENTLEMAN stays behind, alone. Then he sits on the divan.)*

YOUNG GENTLEMAN: *(Smiles and says to himself.)* Finally! An affair with a respectable woman!

(END OF THE SCENE)

\*\*\*\*

# THE READING ROOM

## YOUNG ACTORS AND THEIR TEACHERS

Allen, R. *An Annotated Arthur Schnitzler Bibliography*. Chapel Hill: The University of North Carolina Press, 1966.

Bithell, J. *Modern German Literature 1880–1950*. London: Methuen, 1959.

Coghlan, B. "The Turn of the Century." *Periods in German Literature*. Vol. 1. J. M. Ritchie, Ed. London: Wolff, 1966.

Pascal, R. *From Naturalism to Expressionism. German Literature and Society 1880–1918*. London: Weidenfels and Nicholson 1973.

## SCHOLARS, STUDENTS, PROFESSORS

Beller, S. *Vienna and the Jews, 1867–1938: A Cultural History*. Cambridge and New York: Cambridge University Press, 1989.

_____, ed. *Rethinking Vienna 1900*. New York: Berghahn Books, 2001.

Boyer, J. *Political Radicalism in Late Imperial Vienna*. Chicago: University of Chicago Press, 1981.

_____. *Culture and Political Crisis in Vienna*. Chicago: University of Chicago Press, 1995.

Broch, H. *Hugo von Hofmannsthal and His Time: The European Imagination, 1860–1920*. Chicago: University of Chicago Press, 1984.

Daviau, D. *Hermann Bahr*. Boston: Twayne Publishers, 1985.

Evans, R. *The Feminist Movement in Germany 1894–1933*. London: Sage Publications, 1976.

Field, F. *The Last Days of Mankind: Karl Kraus and His Vienna*. London: Macmillan, 1967.

Fischer, J. *Fin de Siècle: Kommentar zu einer Epoche*. Munich: Winkler, 1978.

---

This extensive bibliography lists books about the playwright according to whom the books might be of interest. If you would like to research further something that interests you in the text, lists of references, sources cited, and editions used in this book are found in this section.

Fuchs, A. *Geistige Strömungen in Osterreich.* Vienna: Löcker, 1978.

Gainham, S. *The Habsburg Twilight.* London: Weidenfels and Nicolson, 1979.

Good, D. *The Economic Rise of the Habsburg Empire, 1750–1914.* Berkeley: University of California Press, 1984.

Janik, A., and S. Toulmin. *Wittgenstein's Vienna.* London: Weidelfels and Nicholson, 1973.

Johnston, W. *The Austrian Mind: An Intellectual and Social History 1848–1938.* Berkeley: University of California Press, 1972.

Lindken, H. *Arthur Schnitzler: Aspekte und Akzente — Materialien zu Leben und Werk.* Bern: Lang, 1984.

Luft, D. S. *Robert Musil and the Crisis of European Culture, 1880–1942.* Berkeley: University of California Press, c. 1980.

May, A. *The Habsburg Monarchy 1867–1914.* Cambridge, Mass.: Harvard University Press, 1965.

Osborne, J. *The Naturalist Drama in Germany.* Manchester, England: Manchester University Press, 1971.

Politzer, H. "Arthur Schnitzler: Poetry of Psychology." *Modern Language Notes* 78, no. 4 (October 1963).

Reichert, H. "Arthur Schnitzler and Modern Ethics." *Journal of the International Arthur Schnitzler Research Association* 2, no. I. (Spring 1963).

Reik, T. *Arthur Schnitzler als Psycholog.* Minden, Germany: J. C. C. Bruns, 1913.

Rieder, H. *Arthur Schnitzler: Das dichterische Werk.* Vienna: Bergland, 1973.

Rudolph, R., and D. Good, eds. *Nationalism and Empire: The Habsburg Empire and the Soviet Union.* New York: St. Martin's Press, 1992.

Scheible, H. *Arthur Schnitzler in Selbstzeugnissen und Bilddokumenten.* Reinbek bei Hamburg, Germany: Rowohlt, 1976.

_____. *Arthur Schnitzler und die Aufklärung.* Munich: W. Fink, 1977.

_____, ed. *Arthur Schnitzler in neuer Sicht.* Munich: W. Fink, 1981.

Schnitzler, H., Brandstätter, and R. Unger. *Arthur Schnitzler: Sein Leben, sein Werk, seine Zeit.* Frankfurt-am-Main, Germany: S. Fischer, 1981.

Seidlin, O. "In Memoriam Arthur Schnitzler: May 15, 1862–October 21, 1931." *American-German Review* 28, no. 4 (April–May, 1962).

Sked, A. *The Decline and Fall of the Habsburg Empire, 1815–1918.* Harlow and New York: Longmans, 2001.

Specht, R. *Arthur Schnitzler: Der Dichter und sein Werk: Eine Studie.* Berlin: S. Fischer, 1922.

Spiel, H. *Vienna's Golden Autumn.* London: Weidenfels and Nicholson, 1987.

Taylor, A. *The Habsburg Monarchy 1809–1918: A History of the Austrian Empire and Austro-Hungary.* London: Hamish Hamilton, 1948.

Timms, E. Karl Kraus. *Apocalyptic Satirist: Culture and Catastrophe in Habsburg Vienna.* New Haven, Conn.: Yale University Press, 1986.

Vasch, B., and R. Wagner. *Wiener Schnitzler-Aufführungen 1891–1970.* Munich: Prestel, 1971.

Wagner, R. *Frauen um Schnitzler.* Vienna: Jugend und Volk, 1980.

_____. *Arthur Schnitzler. Eine Biographie.* Frankfurt-am-Main, Germany: S. Fischer, 1984.

## THEATERS, PRODUCERS

Barea, I. *Vienna: Legend and Reality.* London: Secker and Warburg, 1966.

Beharriell, F. "Arthur Schnitzler's Range of Theme." *Monatshefte für deutschen Unterricht* 43, no. 7 (November 1951).

Bentley, E. *The Playwright as Thinker: A Study of Drama in Modern Times.* New York: Harcourt, Brace, 1951.

Kann, R. "Schnitzler as an Austrian Writer in the World Today." *Journal of the International Arthur Schnitzler Research Association* I, nos. 4–5 (Autumn–Winter 1962).

Klaus, H. *The Theater Director Otto Brahm.* Ann Arbor: University of Michigan Press, 1981.

## ACTORS, DIRECTORS, THEATER PROFESSIONALS

Bailey, J. "Arthur Schnitzler's Dramatic Works." *Texas Review* 5, no. 4 (July 1920).

Schnitzler, A. *My Youth in Vienna.* New York: Holt, Rinehart and Winston, 1970.

Weiss, R. "The Human Element in the Works of Arthur Schnitzler." *Modern Austrian Literature* 5 (1972).

Williams, C. The Broken Eagle. *The Politics of Austrian Literature from Empire to Anschluss.* London: Elek, 1974.

## THE EDITIONS OF SCHNITZLER'S WORKS USED FOR THIS BOOK

*Arthur Schnitzler: Four Major Plays [La Ronde, Anatol, The Green Cockatoo, Flirtation].* Translated by Carl R. Mueller. Lyme, N.H.: Smith and Kraus, 2000.

## SOURCES CITED IN THIS BOOK

Crankshaw, E. *Vienna: The Image of a Culture in Decline.* London: Macmillan, 1938.

_____. *The Fall of the House of Habsburg.* London: Longmans, 1963.

Gay, Peter. *Schnitzler's Century: The Making of the Middle-Class Culture, 1815–1914.* New York: W. W. Norton, 2002.

Morton, F. *A Nervous Splendor: Vienna 1888–1889.* London: Weidenfels and Nicholson, 1980.

Schorske, C. *Fin de Siècle Vienna: Politics and Culture.* London: Weidenfels and Nicholson, 1980.

Skrine, P. *Hauptmann, Wedekind and Schnitzler.* Basingstoke and London: Macmillan, 1989.

Swales, M. *Arthur Schnitzler: A Critical Study.* Oxford: Clarendon, 1971.

Thompson, Bruce. *Schnitzler's Vienna: Image of a Society.* London, New York: Routledge. 1990.

Urbach, R. *Arthur Schnitzler.* New York: Frederick Ungar, 1973.

# INDEX

---

The entries in the index include highlights from the main In an Hour essay portion of the book.

## ABOUT THE AUTHOR

**Carl Mueller** was a professor in the Department of Theater at the University of California, Los Angeles, from 1967 until his death in 2008. There he directed and taught theater history, criticism, dramatic literature, and playwriting. He was educated at Northwestern University, where he received a B.S. in English. After work in graduate English at the University of California, Berkeley, he received his M.A. in Playwriting at UCLA, where he also completed his Ph.D. in Theater History and Criticism. In 1960–1961 he was a Fulbright Scholar in Berlin.

A translator for more than forty years, he translated and published works by Büchner, Brecht, Wedekind, Hauptmann, Hofmannsthal, and Hebbel, to name a few. His published translation of von Horváth's *Tales from the Vienna Woods* was given its London West End premiere in July 1999. For Smith and Kraus he translated individual volumes of plays by Schnitzler, Strindberg, Pirandello, Kleist, and Wedekind. His translation of Goethe's *Faust Part One* and *Part Two* appeared in 2004. He also translated for Smith and Kraus *Sophokles: The Complete Plays* (2000), a two-volume *Aeschylus: The Complete Plays* (2002), and a four-volume *Euripides: The Complete Plays* (2005). His translations have been performed in every English-speaking country and have appeared on BBC-TV.

Smith and Kraus would like to thank Hugh Denard, whose enlightened permissions policy reflects an understanding that copyright law is intended to both protect the rights of creators of intellectual property as well as to encourage its use for the public good.

# Know the playwright, love the play.

Open a new door to theater study, performance, and audience satisfaction with these Playwrights In an Hour titles.

ANCIENT GREEK

Aeschylus   Aristophanes   Euripides   Sophocles

RENAISSANCE

William Shakespeare

MODERN

Anton Chekhov   Noël Coward   Lorraine Hansberry
Henrik Ibsen   Arthur Miller   Molière   Eugene O'Neill
Arthur Schnitzler   George Bernard Shaw   August Strindberg
Frank Wedekind   Oscar Wilde   Thornton Wilder
Tennessee Williams

CONTEMPORARY

Edward Albee   Alan Ayckbourn   Samuel Beckett
Theresa Rebeck   Sarah Ruhl   Sam Shepard   Tom Stoppard
August Wilson

To purchase or for more information
visit our web site inanhourbooks.com